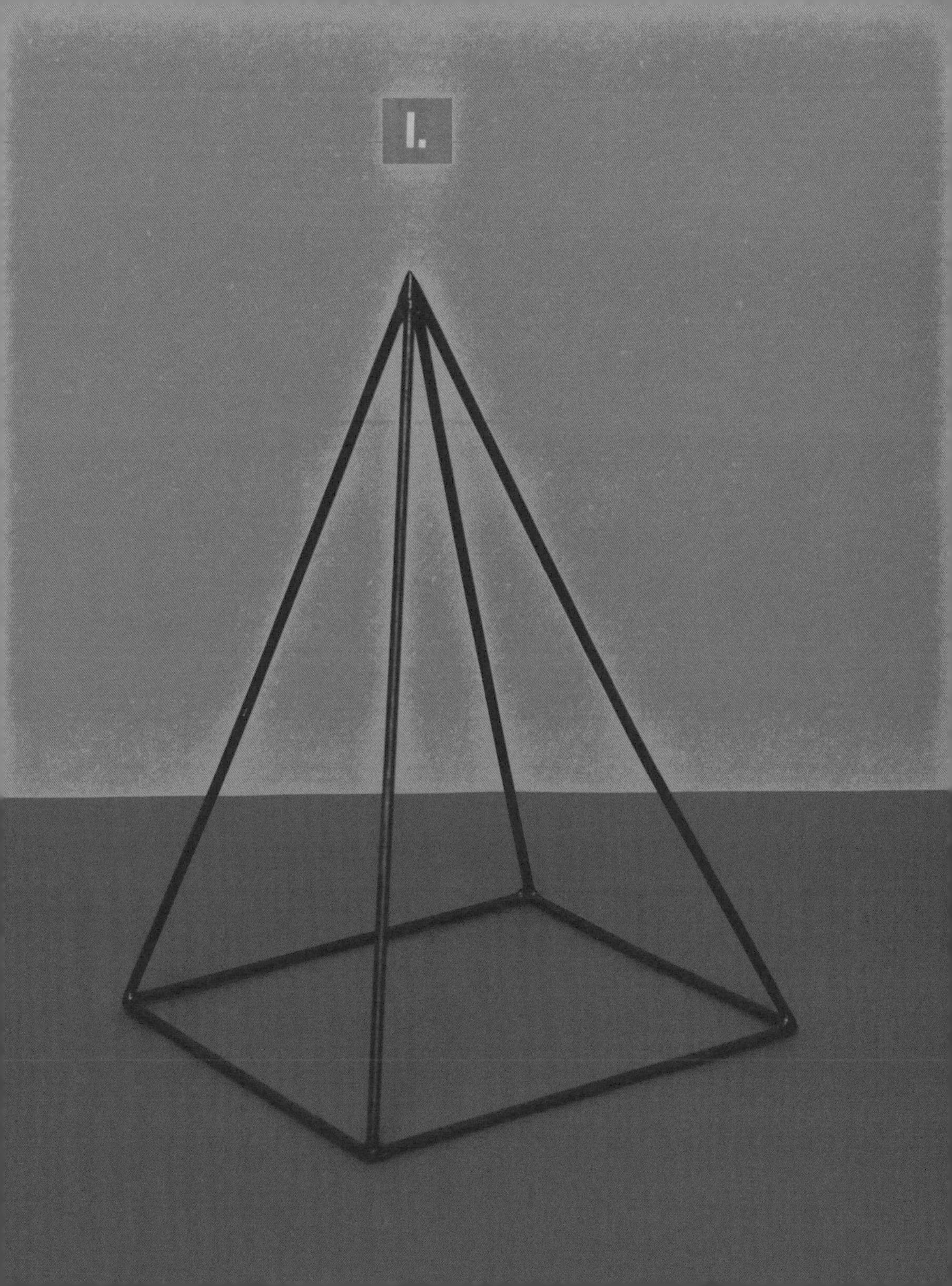
I.

THE FIRST MARCH OF GENTLEMEN

RAFAŁ MILACH

GOST

II.

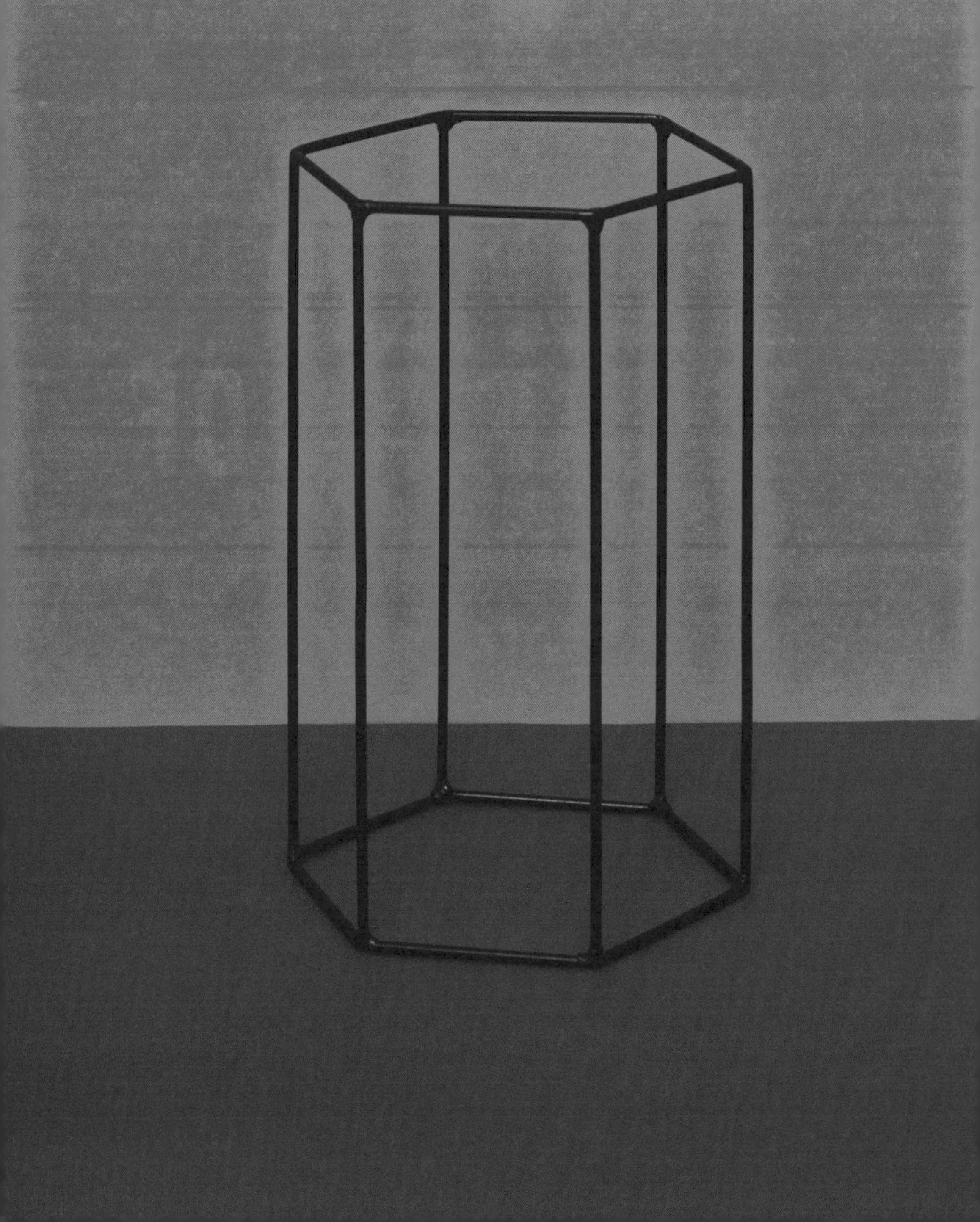

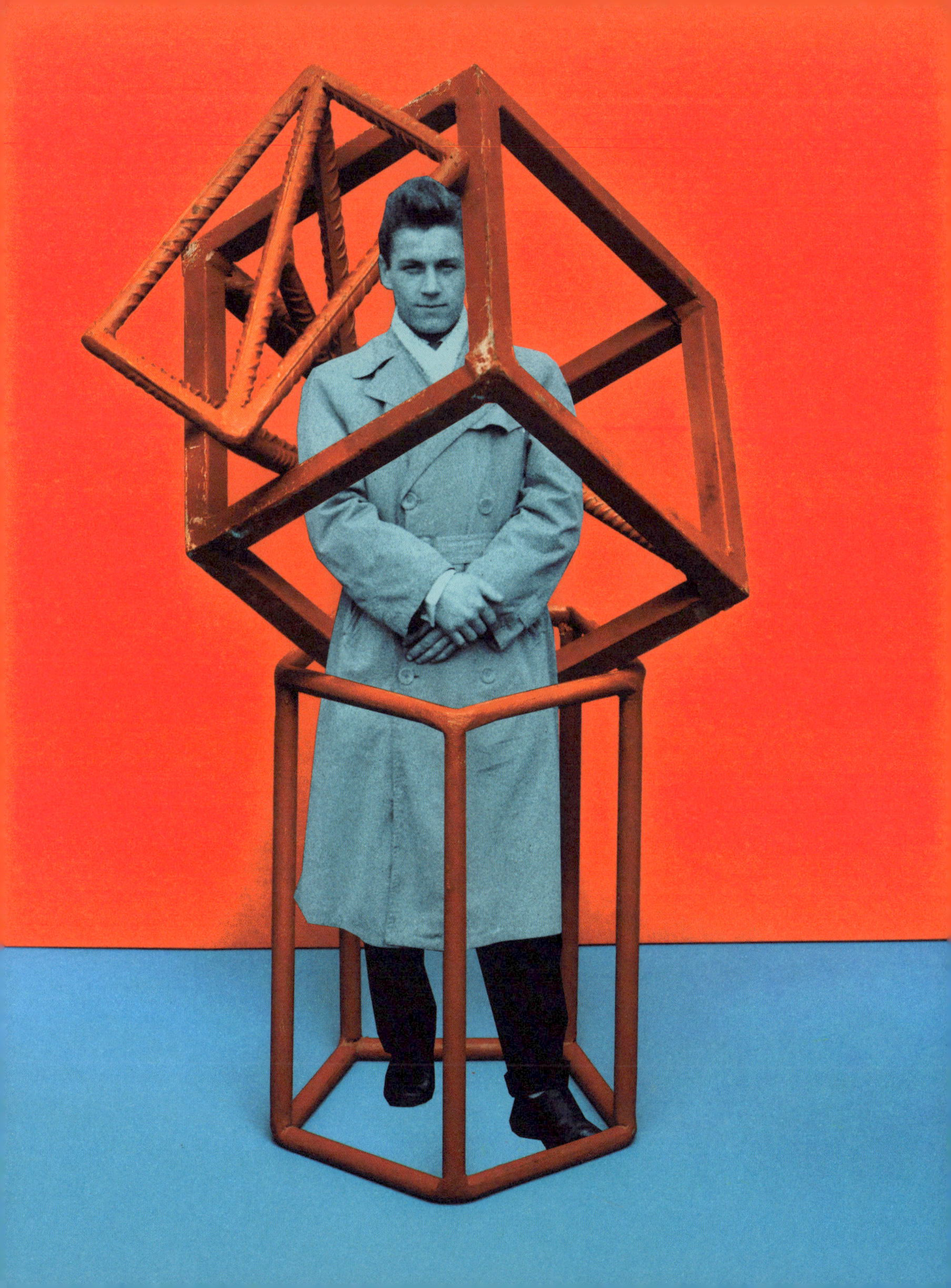

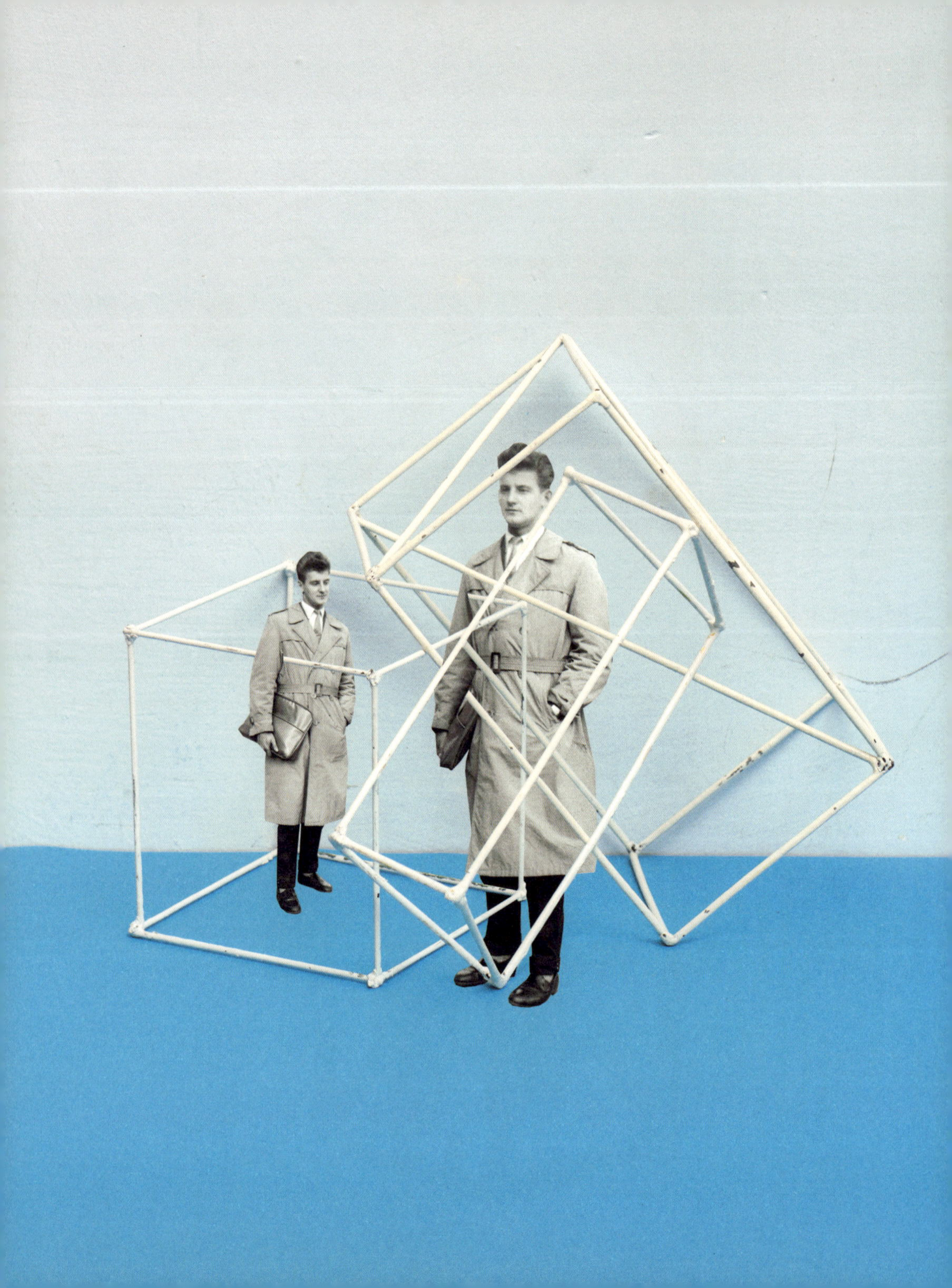

III.

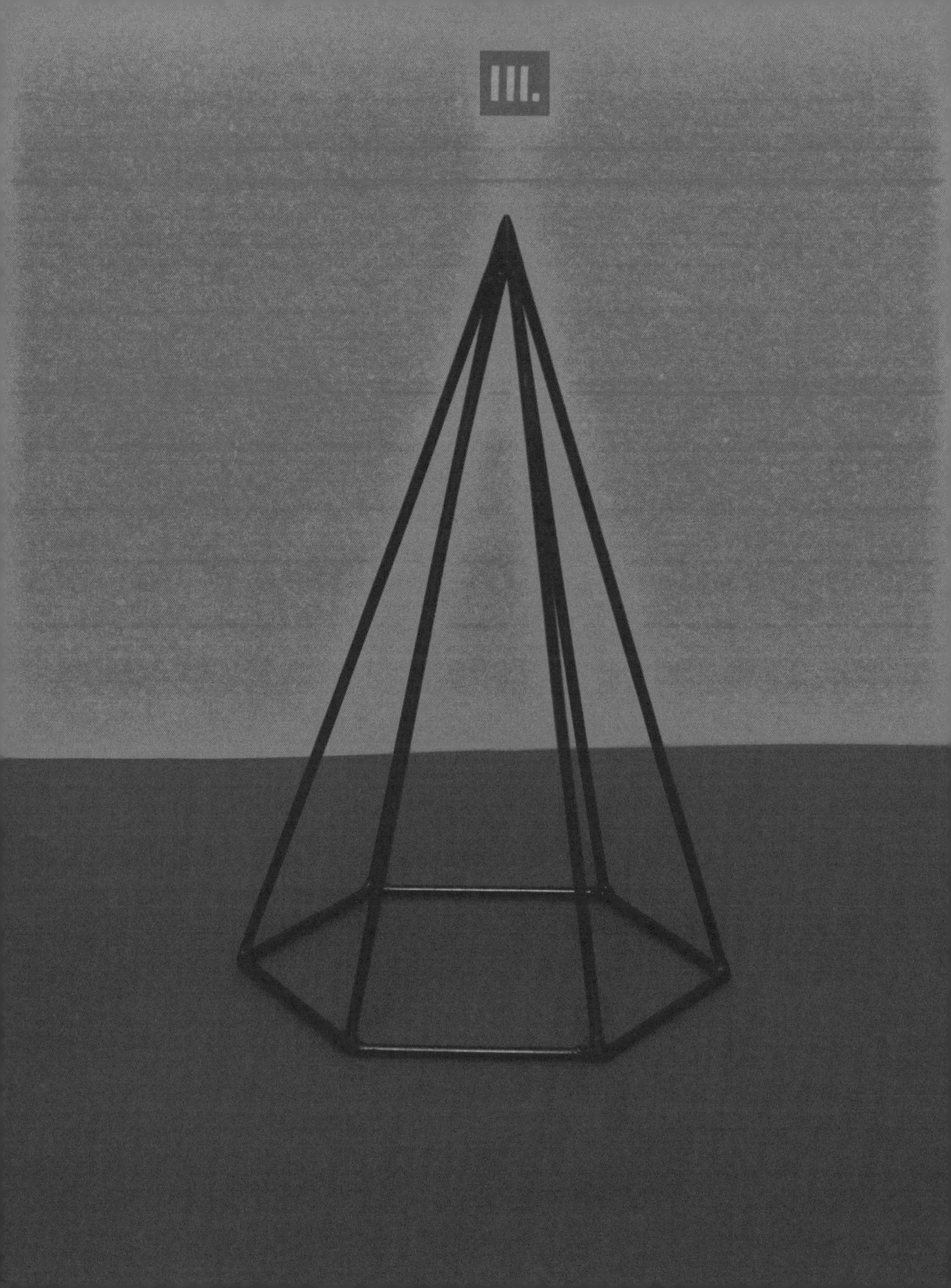

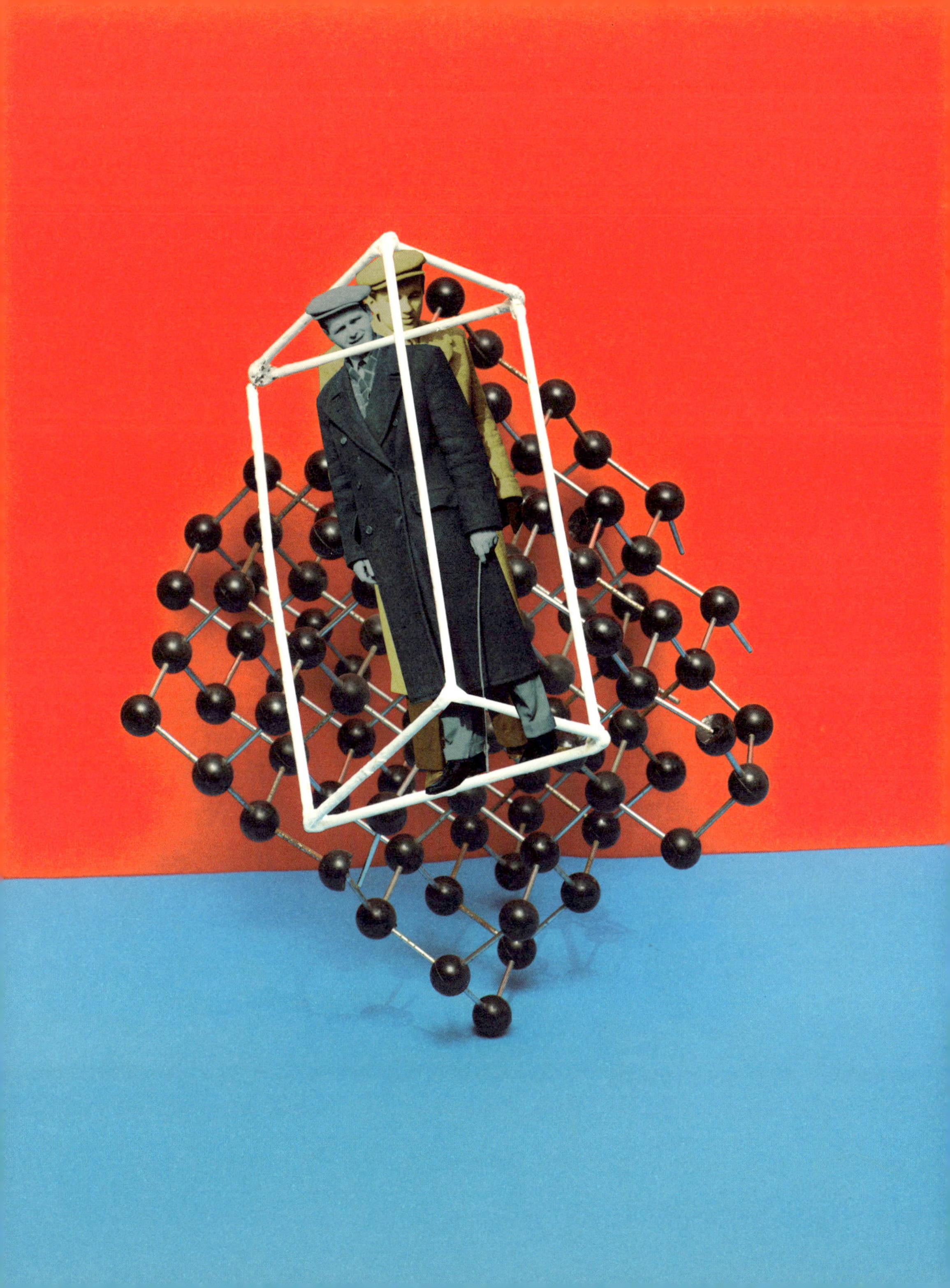

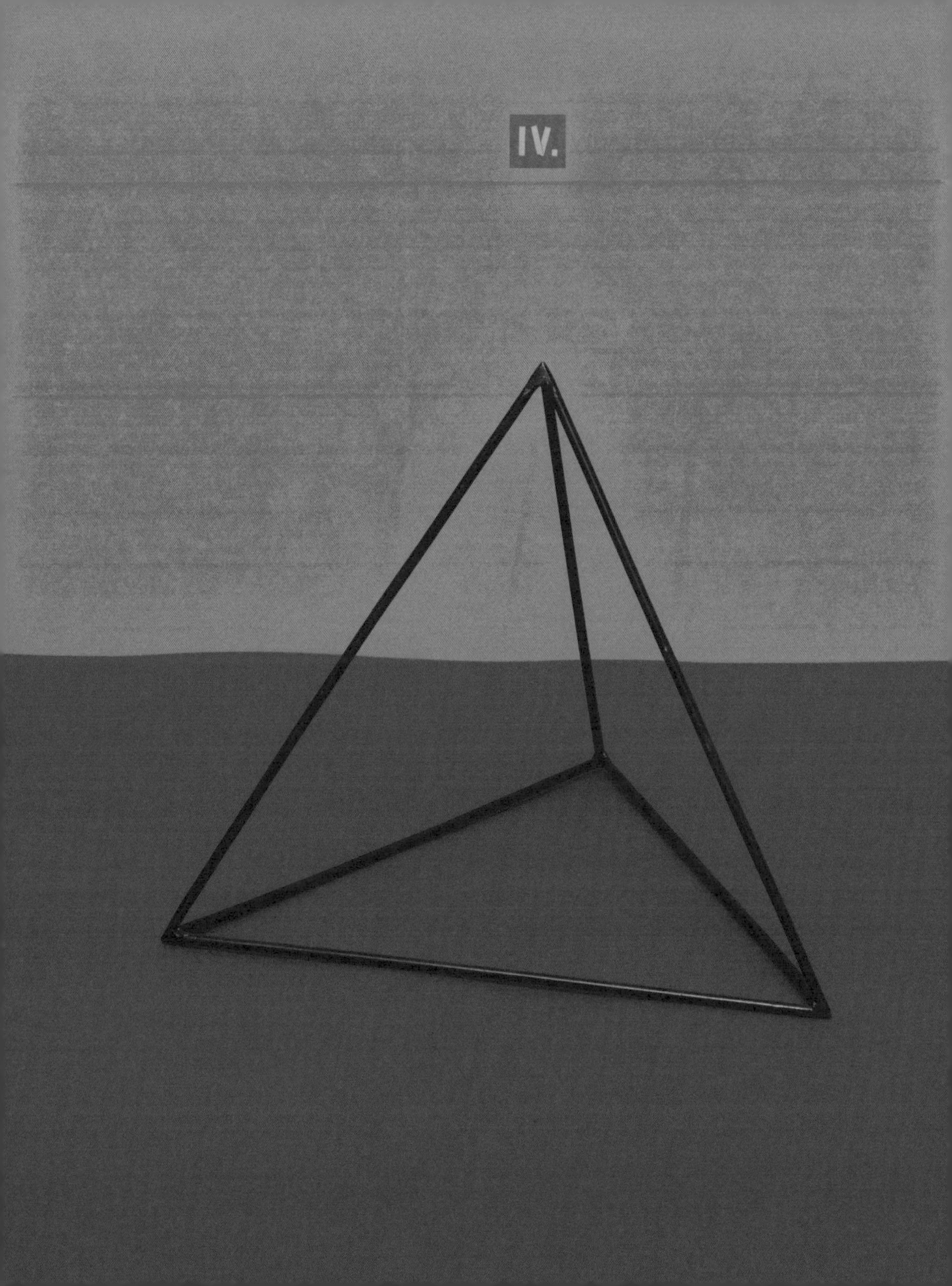
IV.

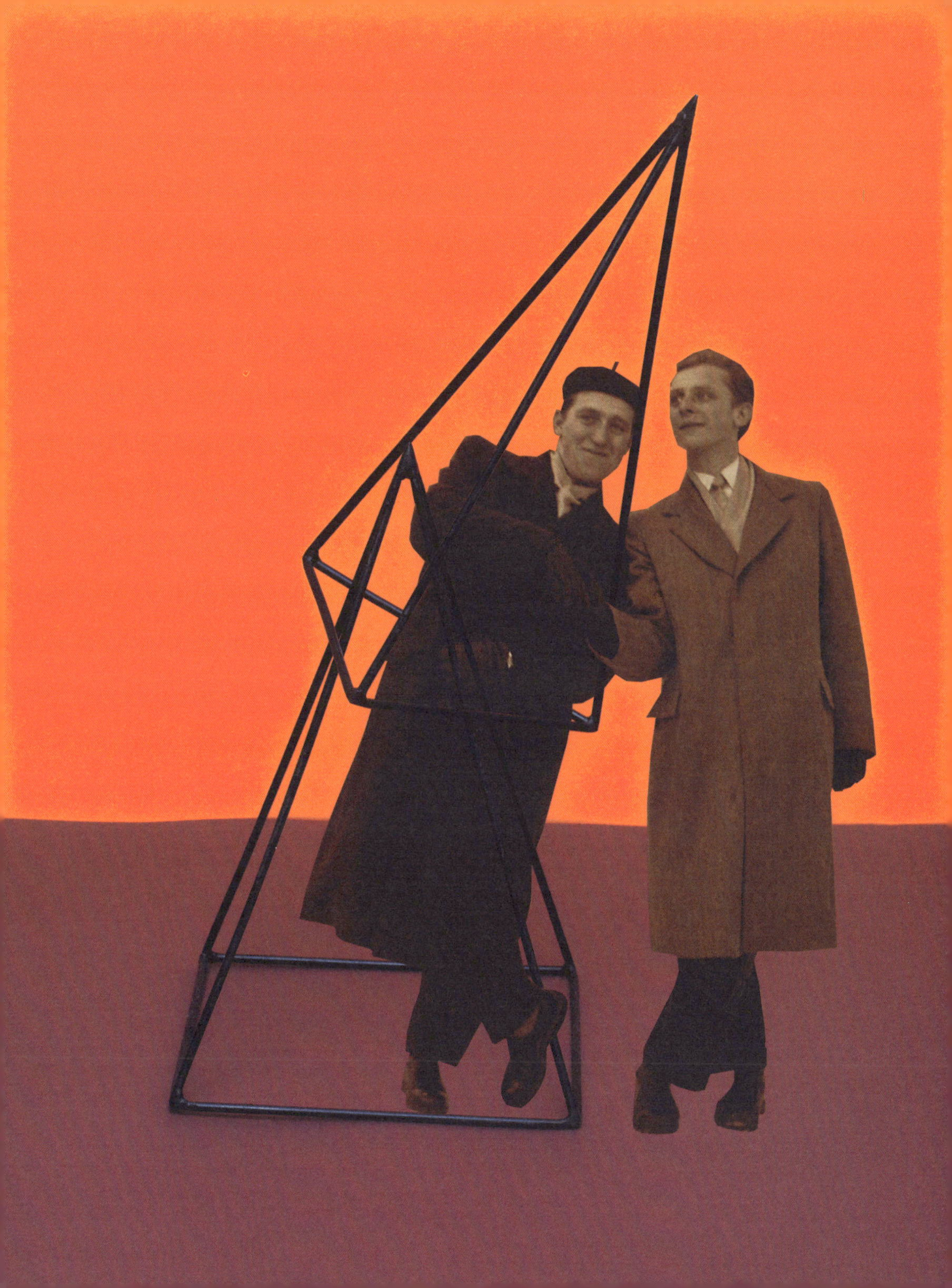

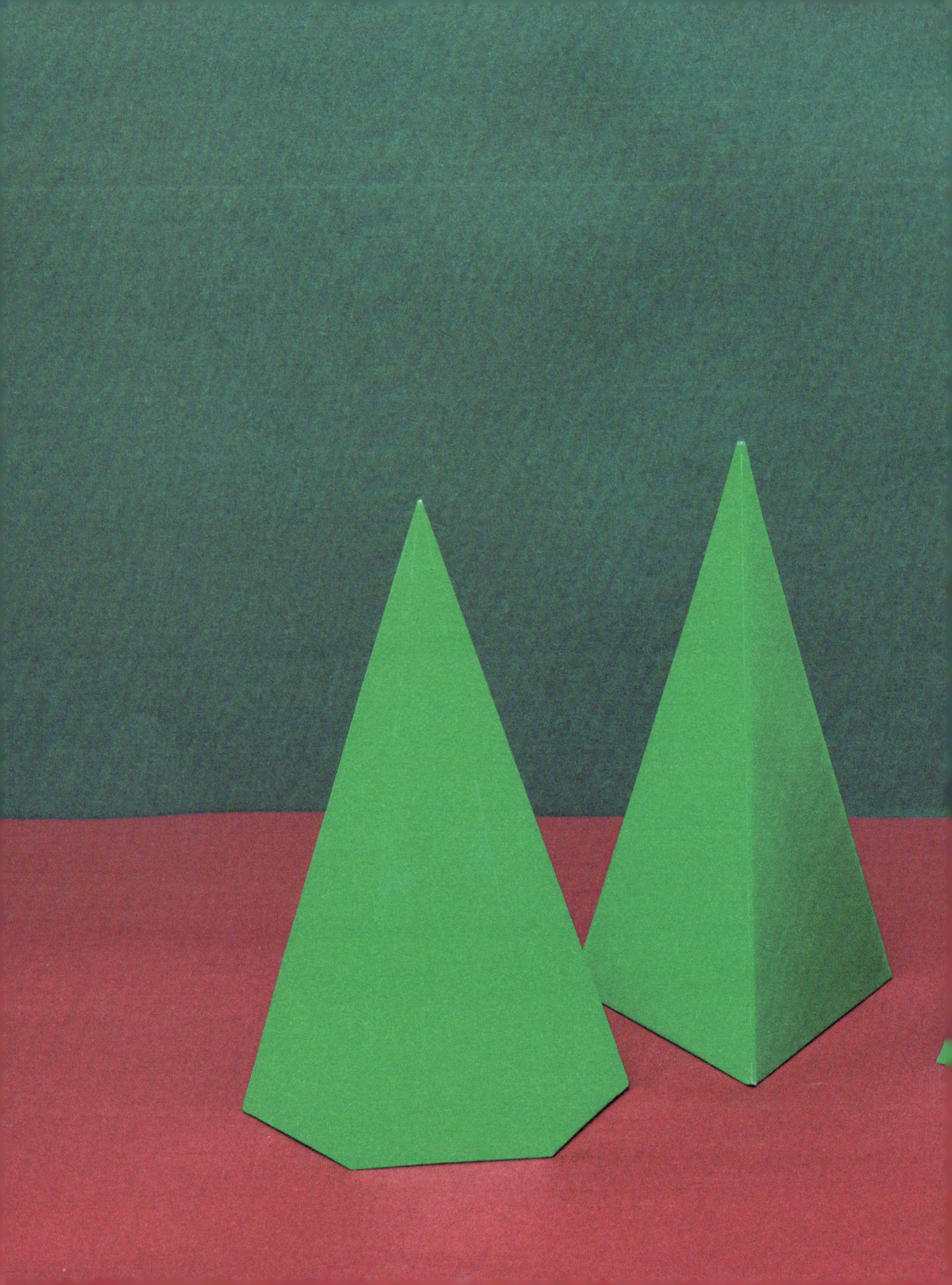

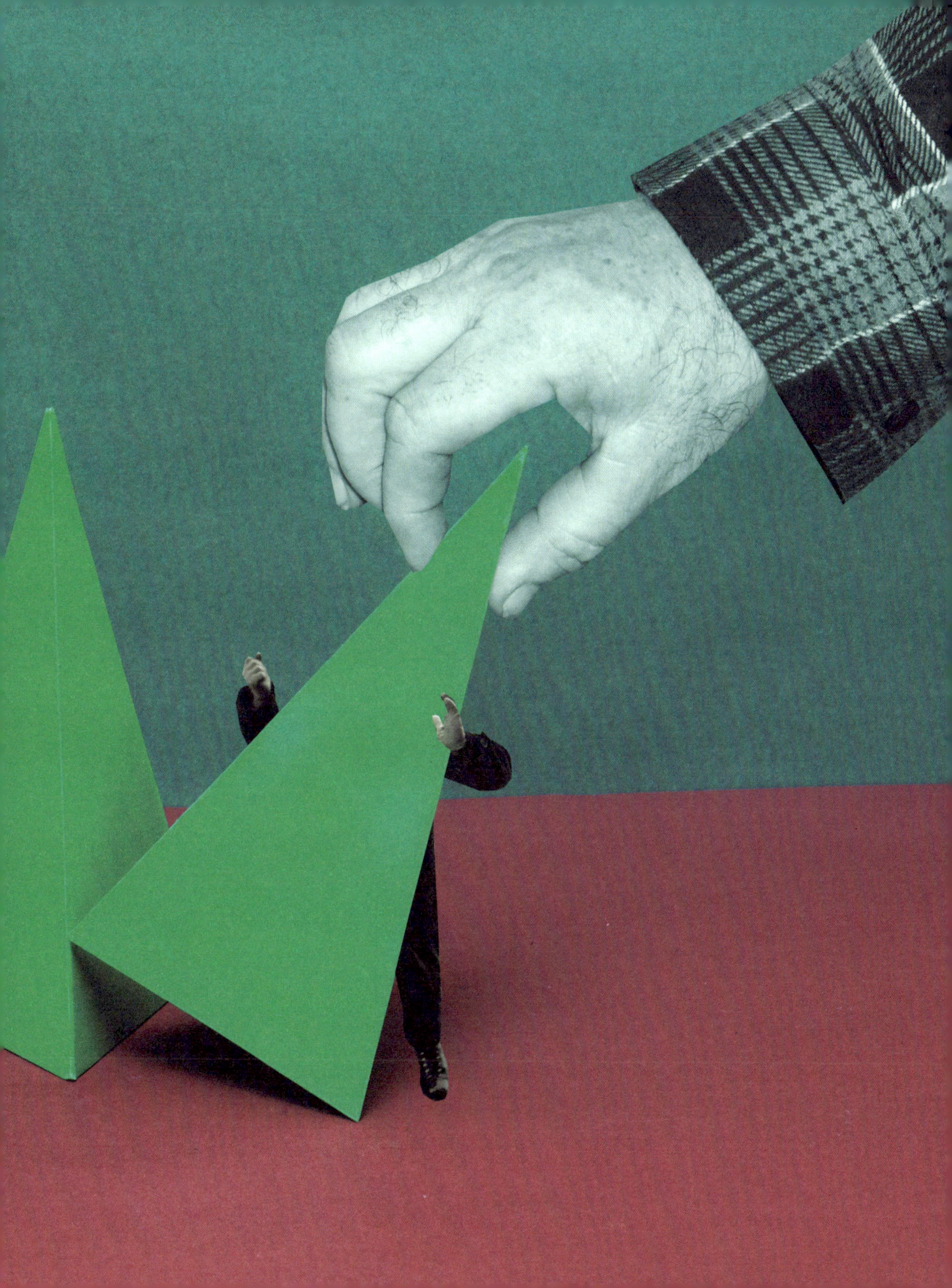

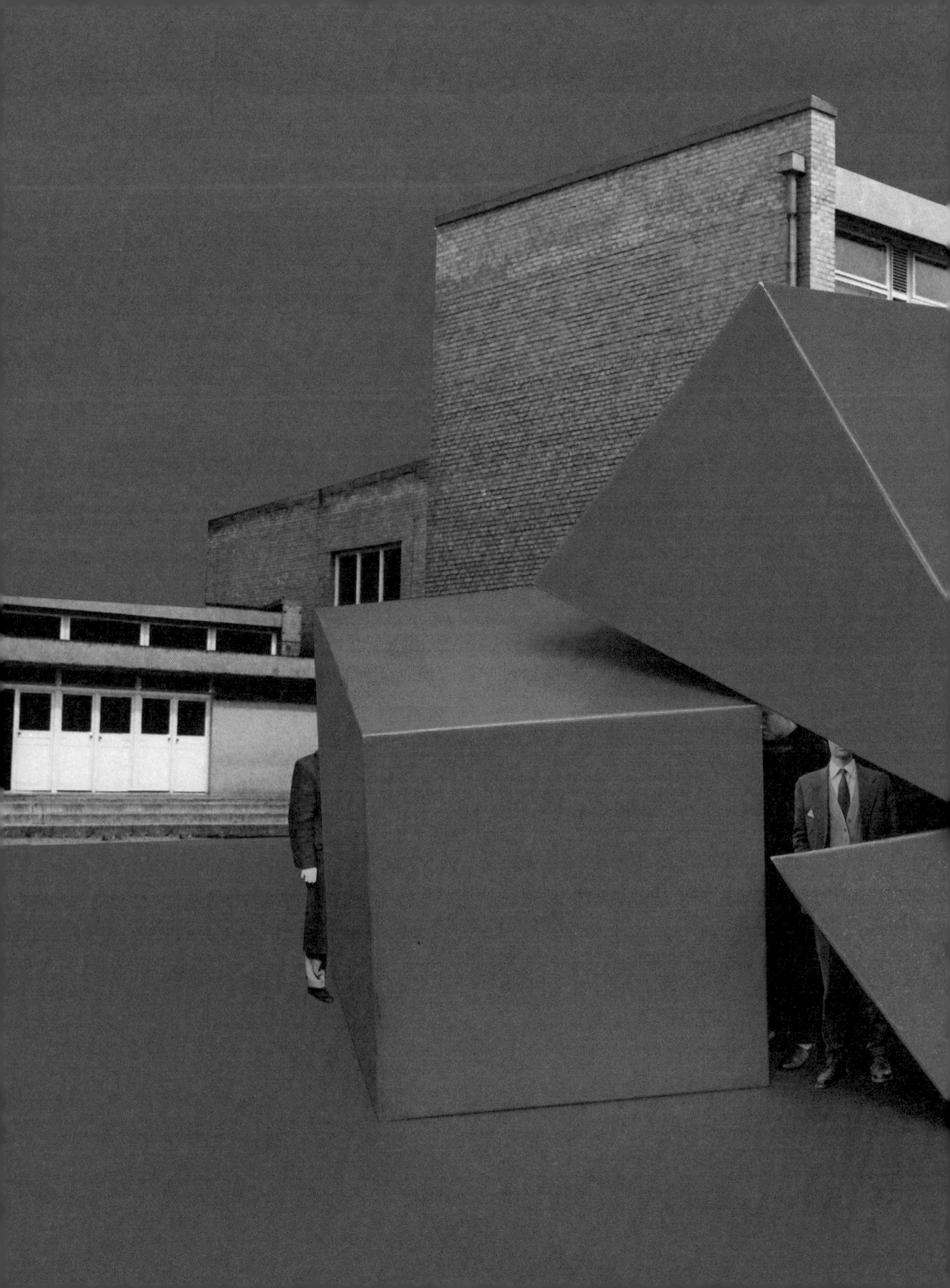

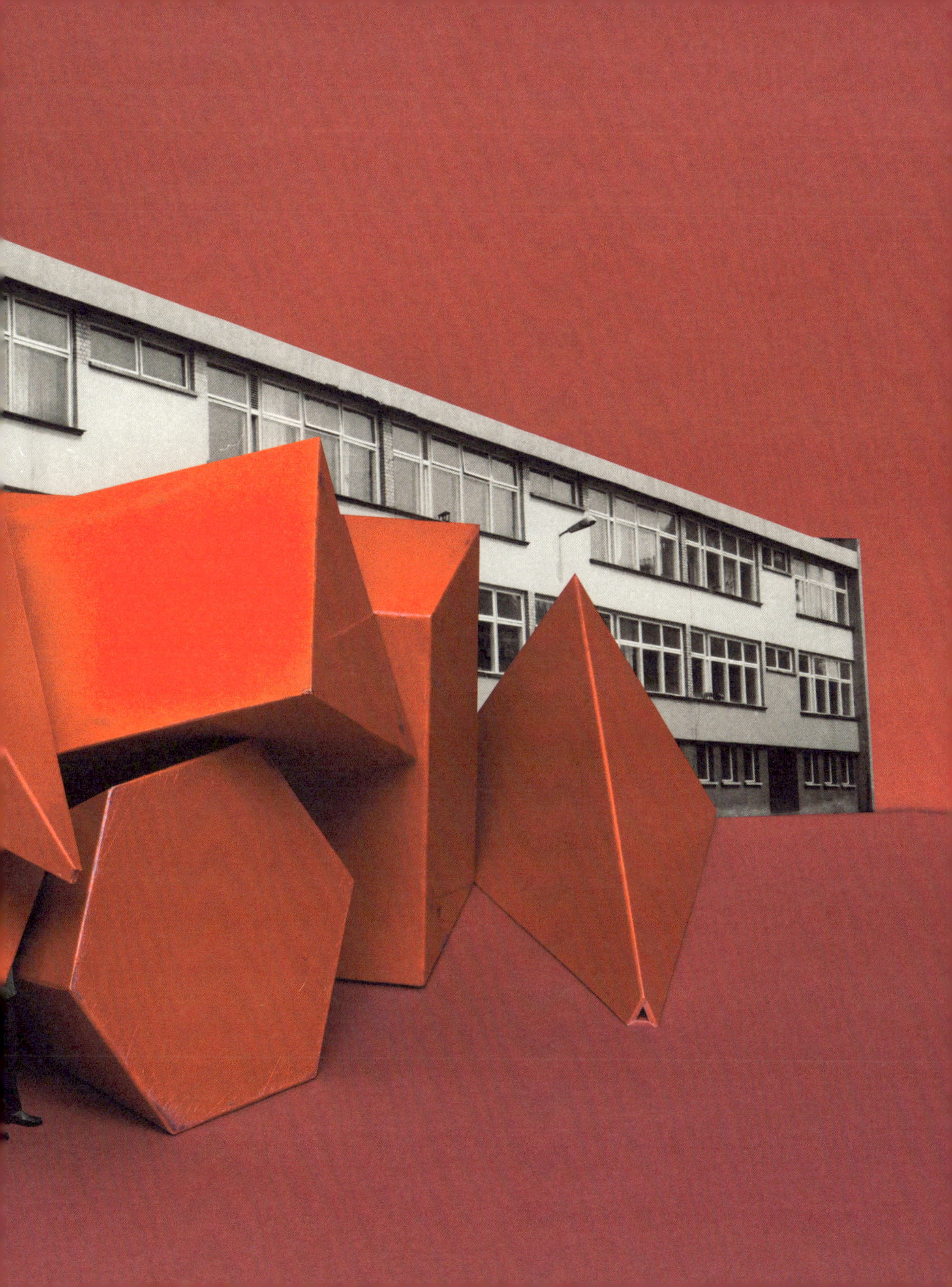

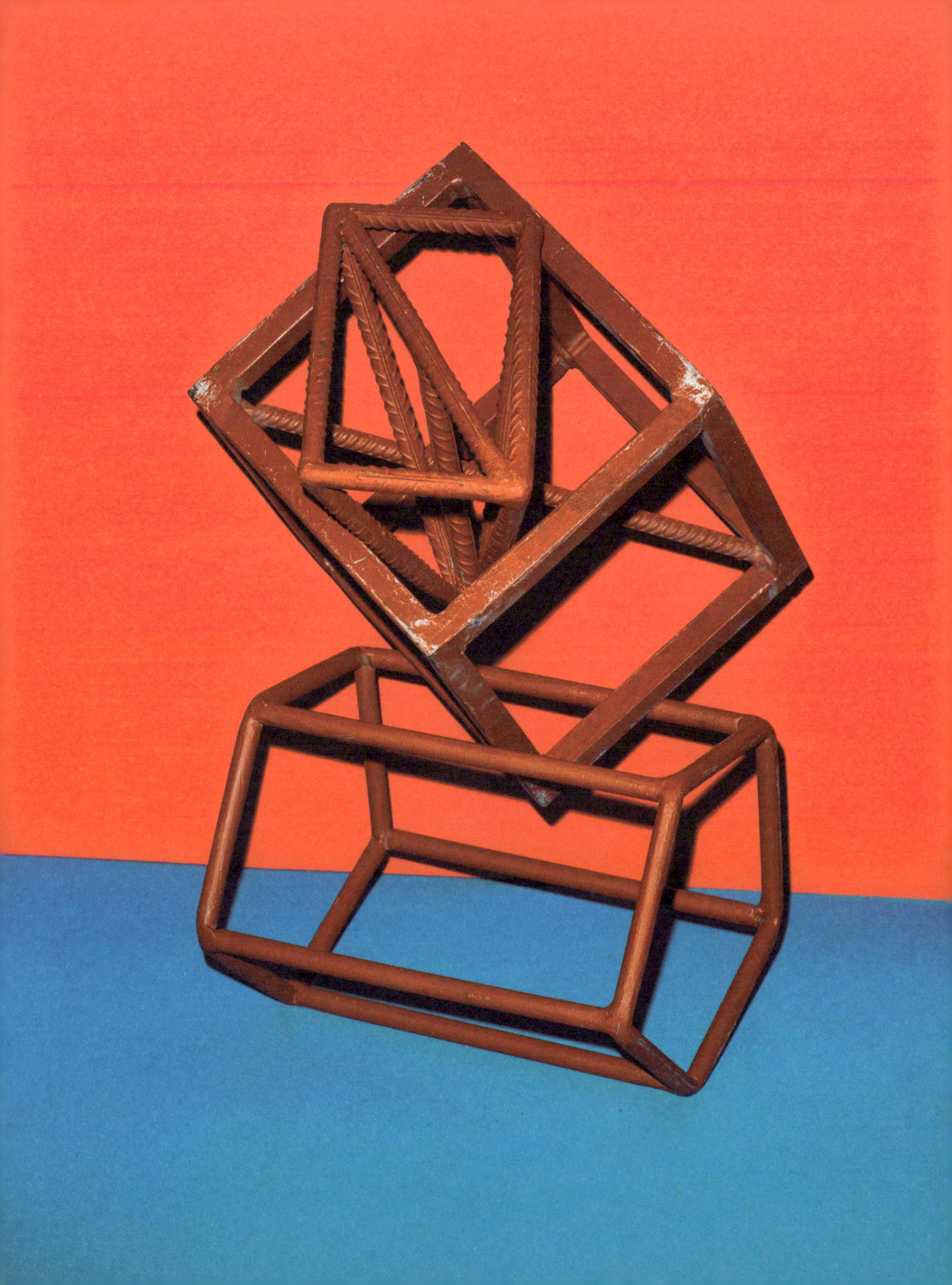

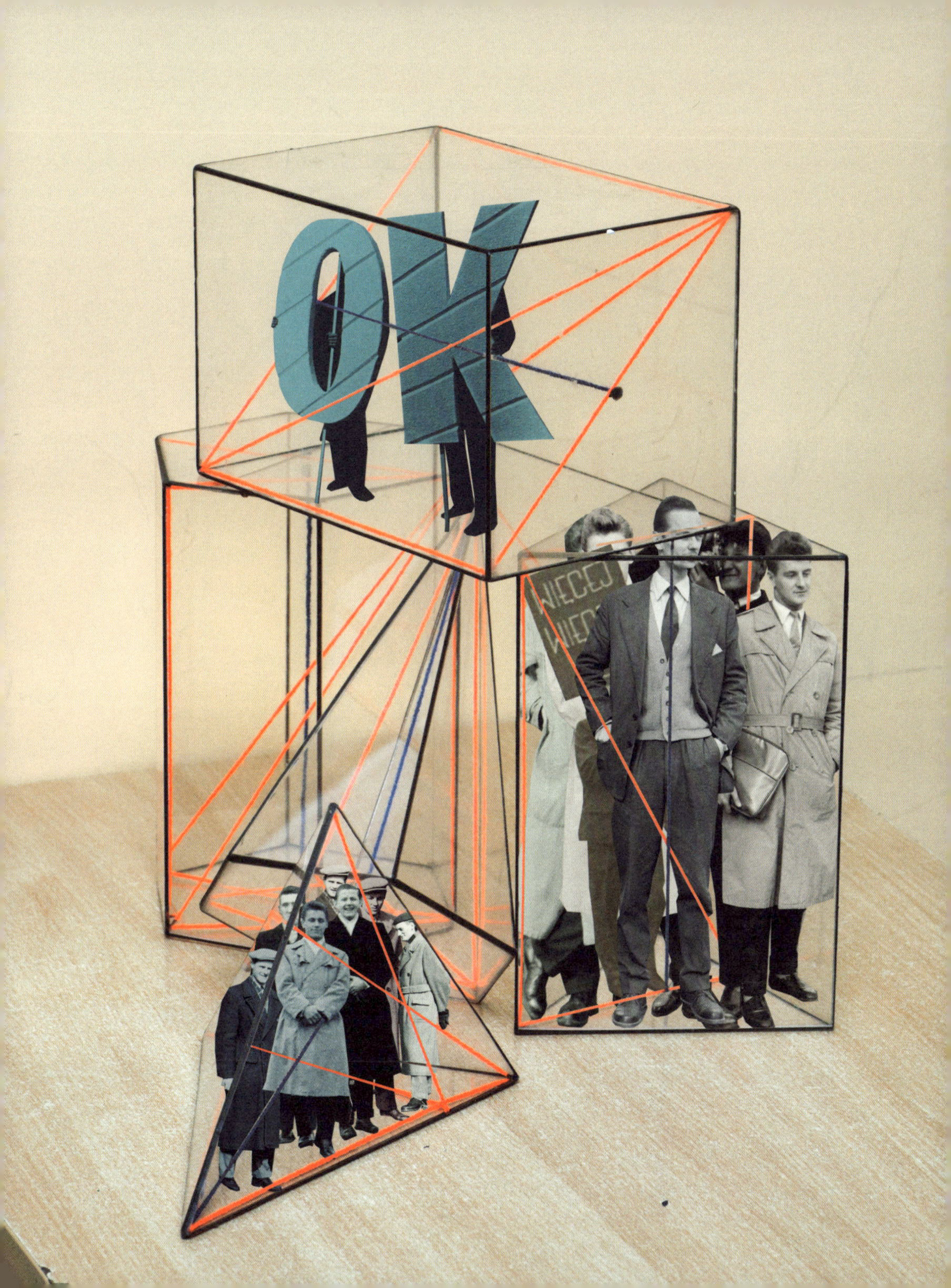
OK
WIĘCEJ

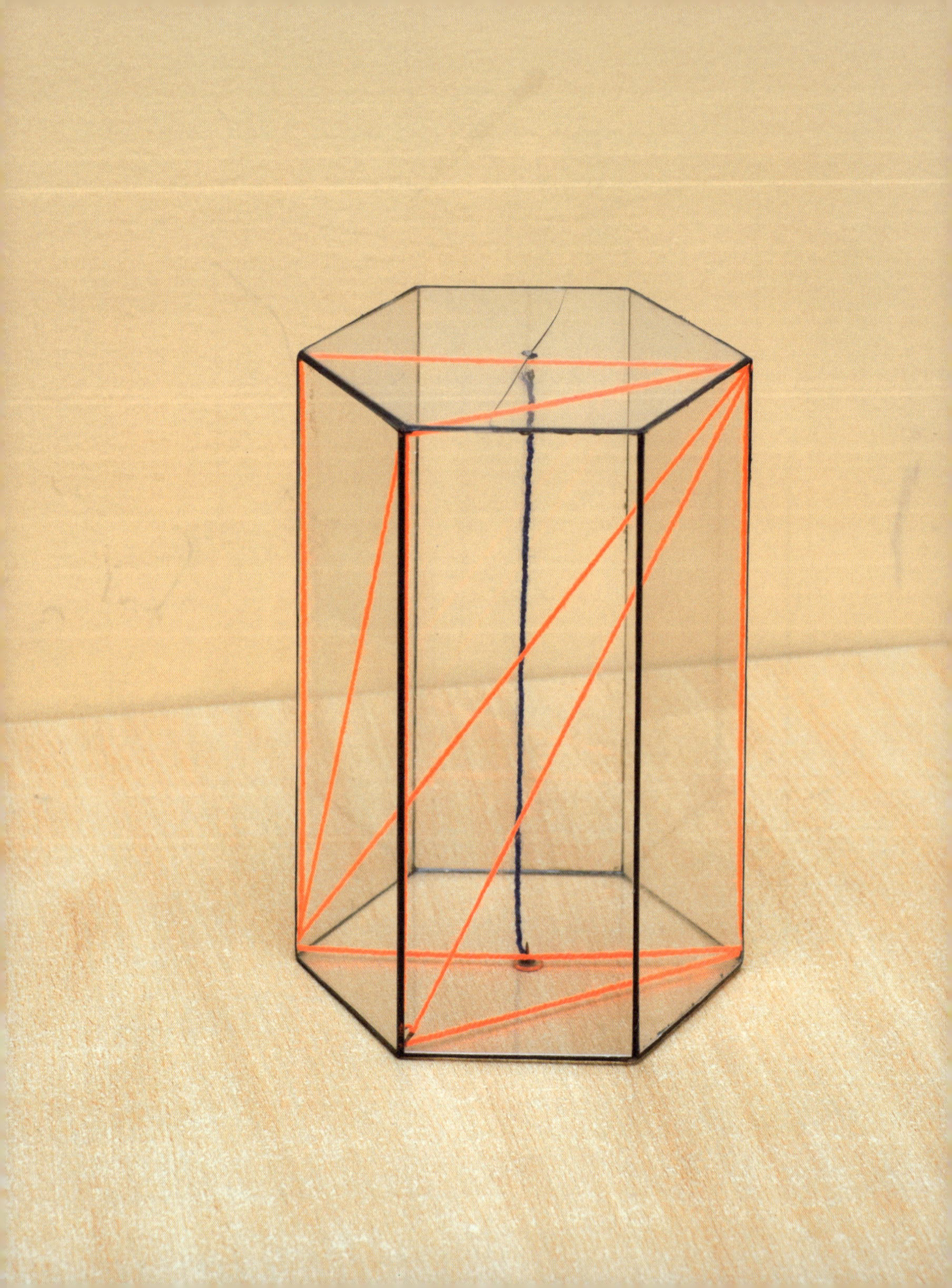

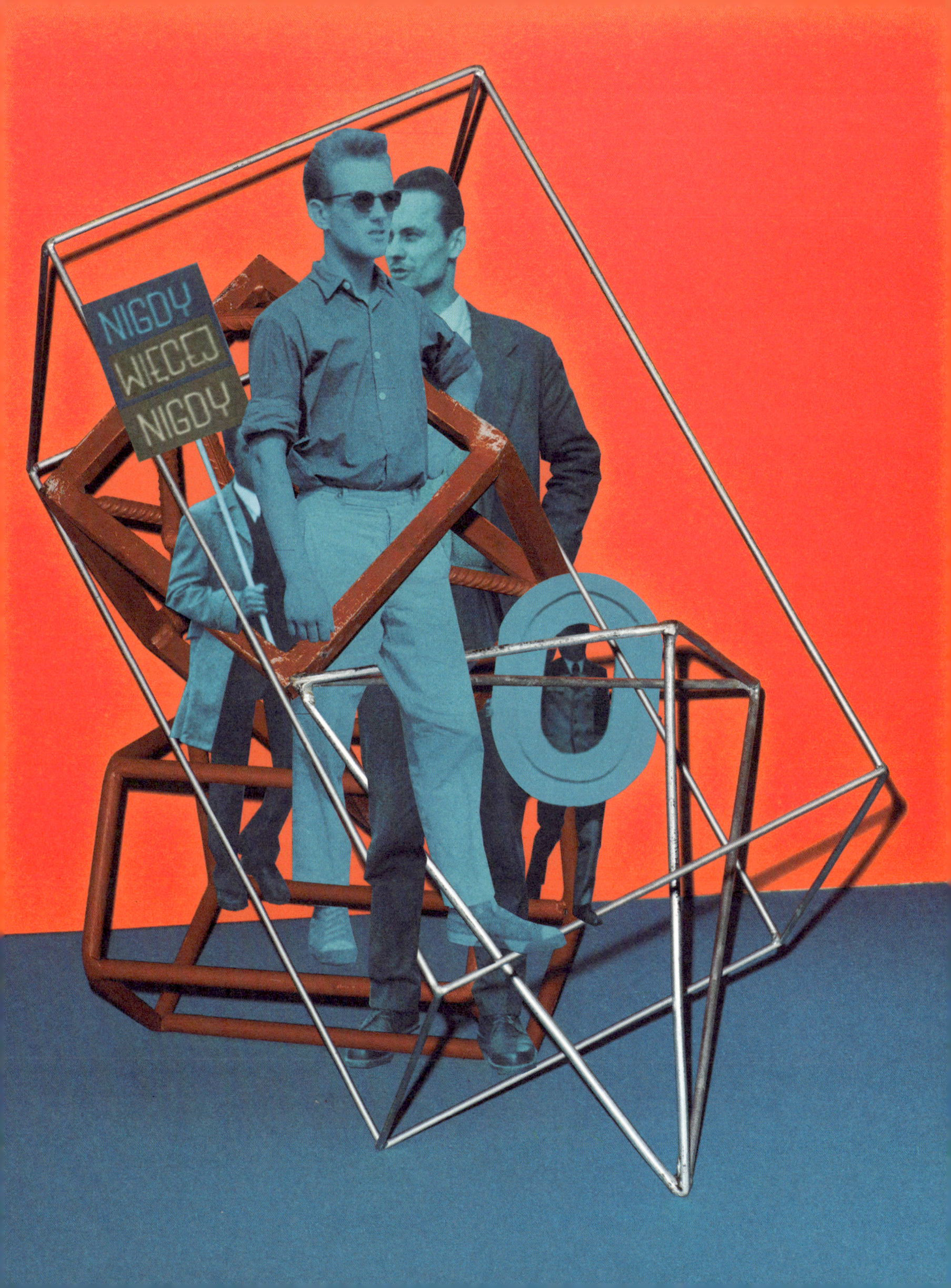
NIGDY
WIĘCEJ
NIGDY

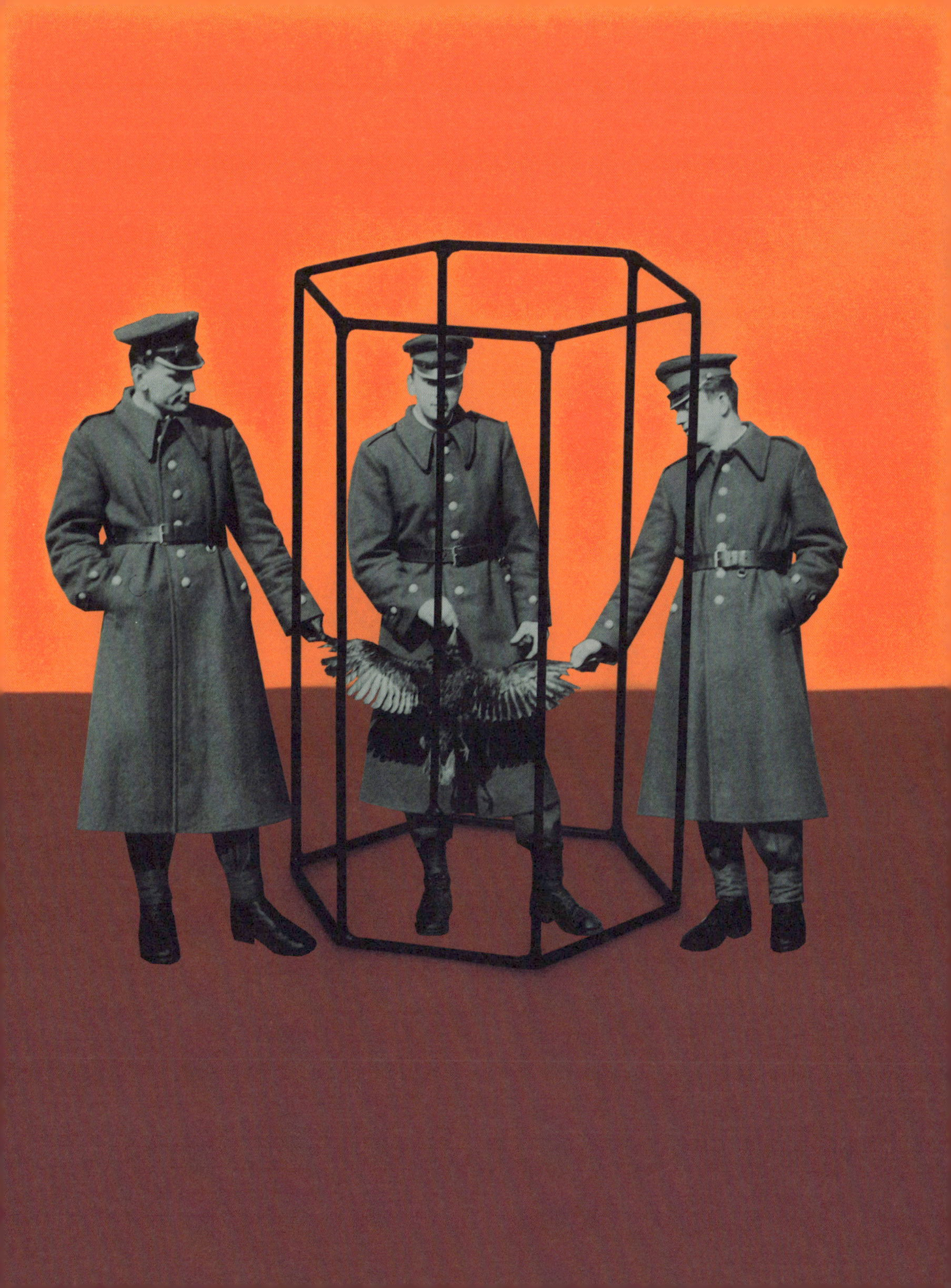

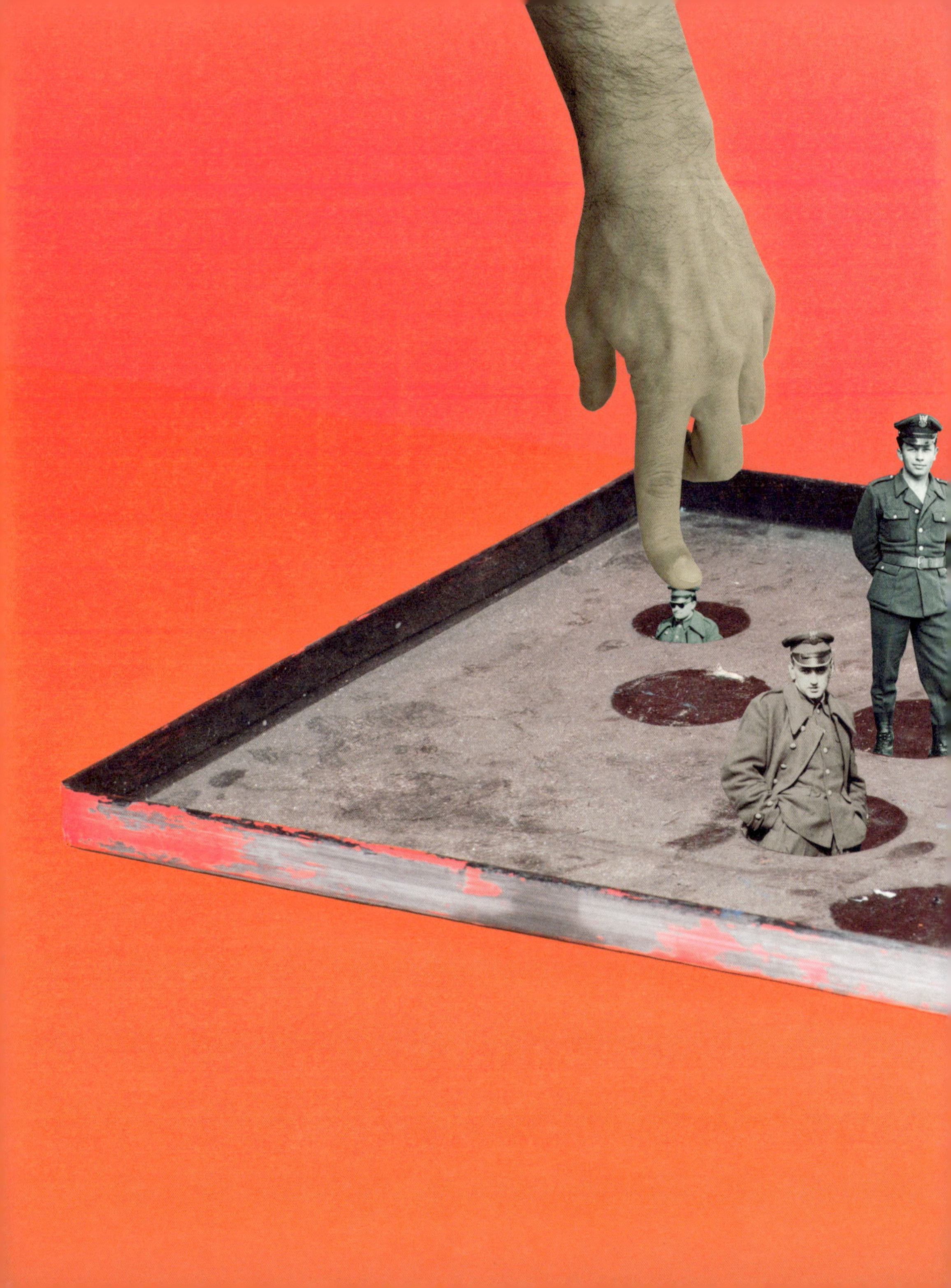

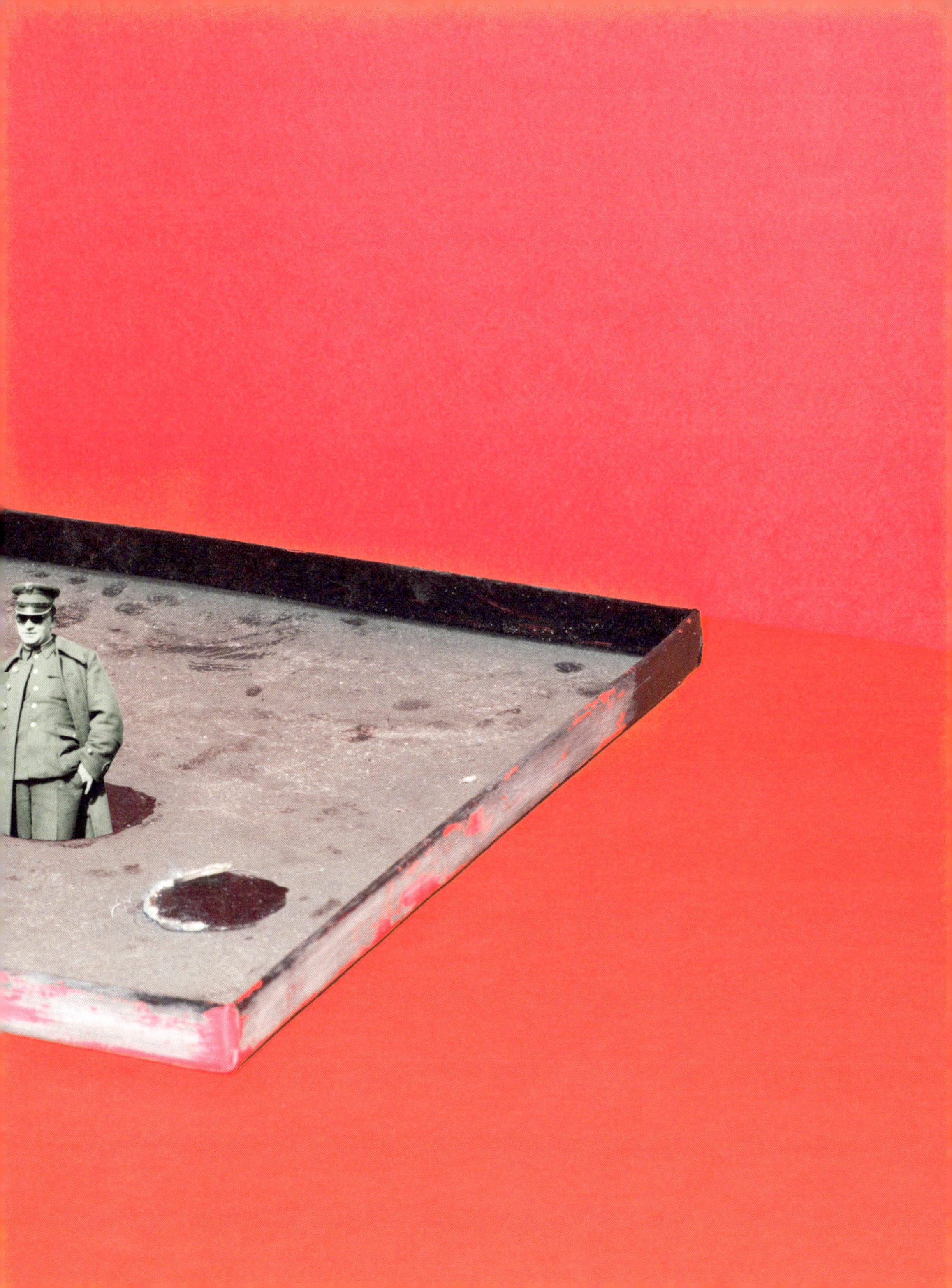

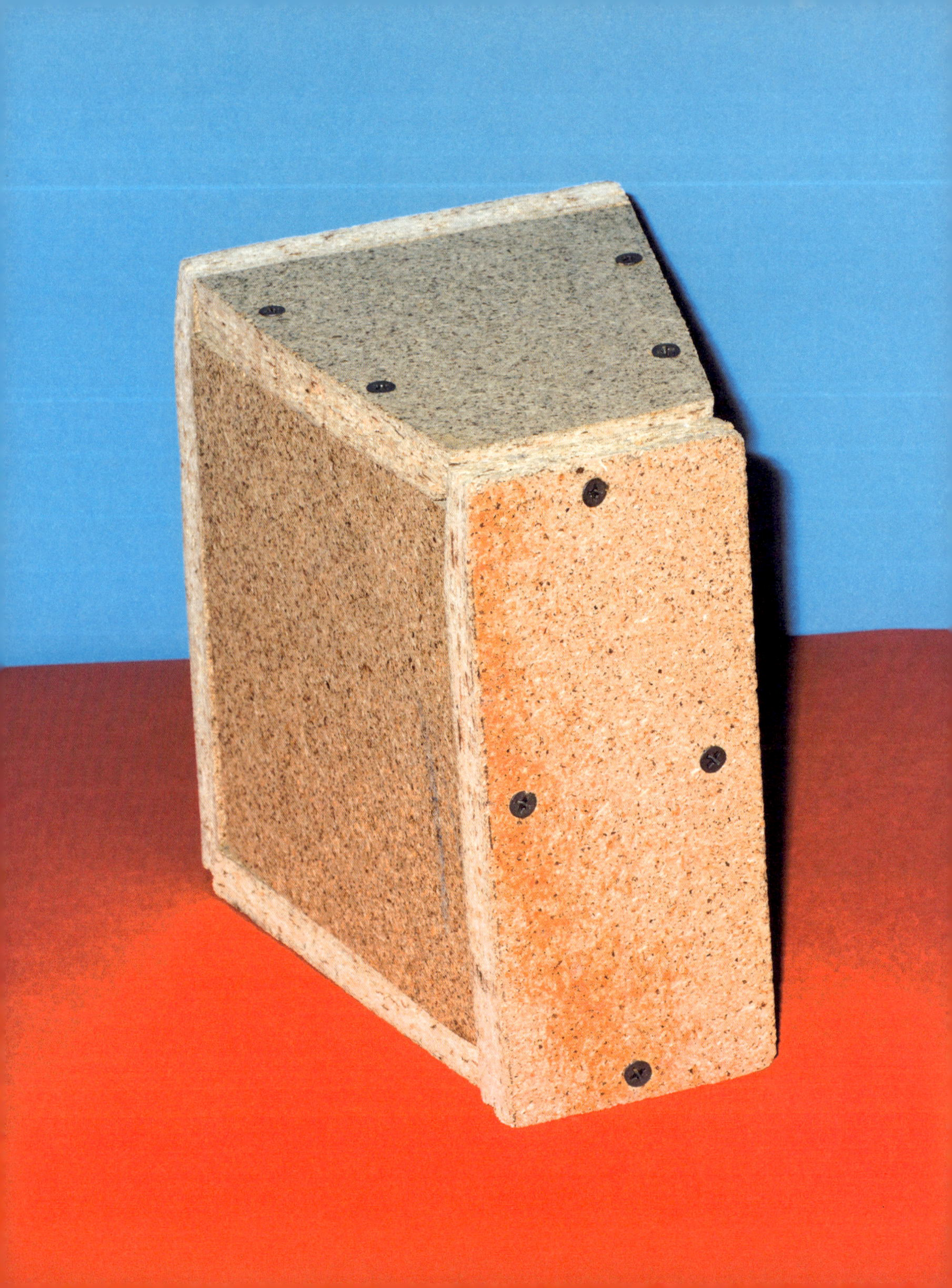

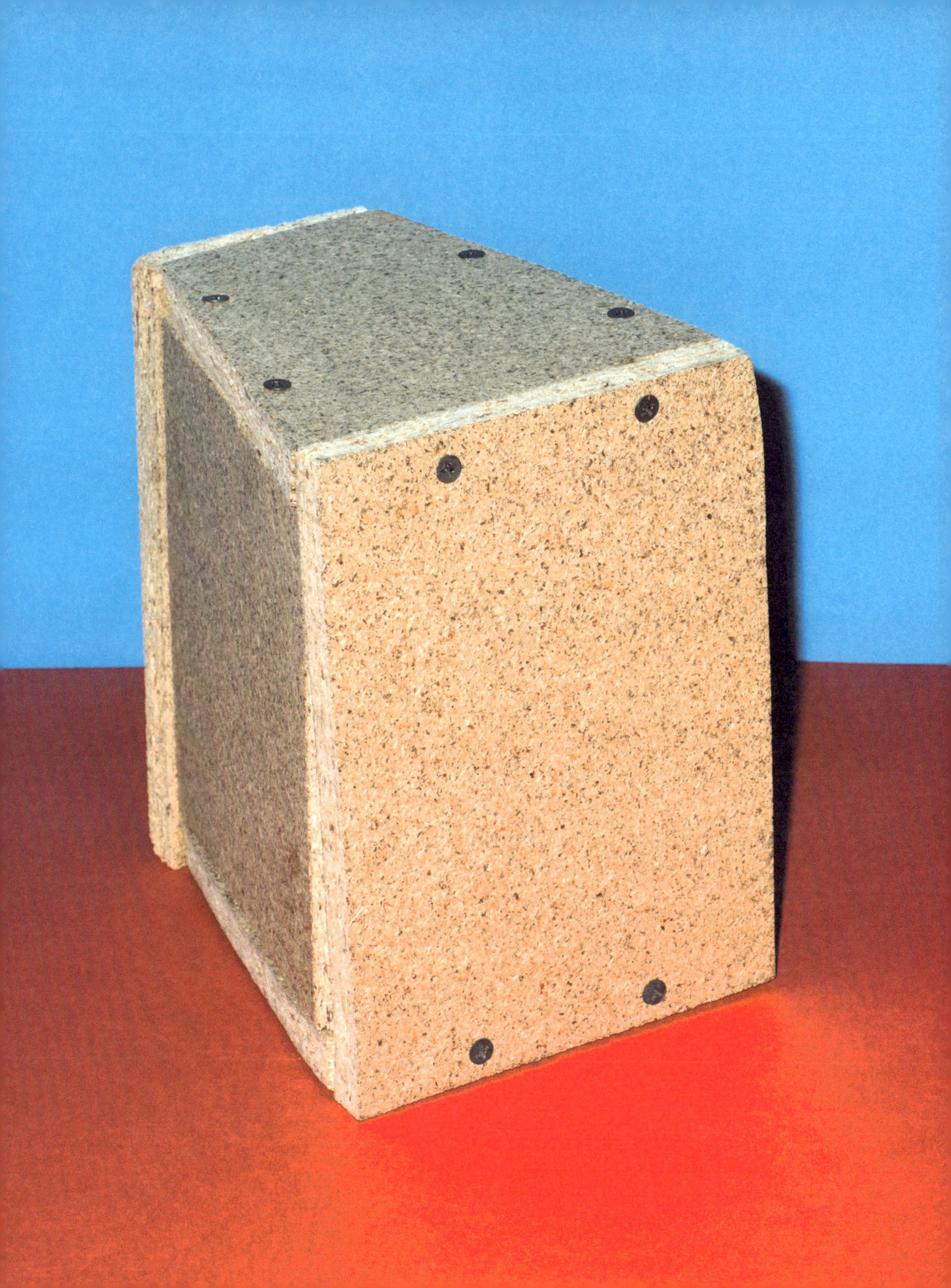

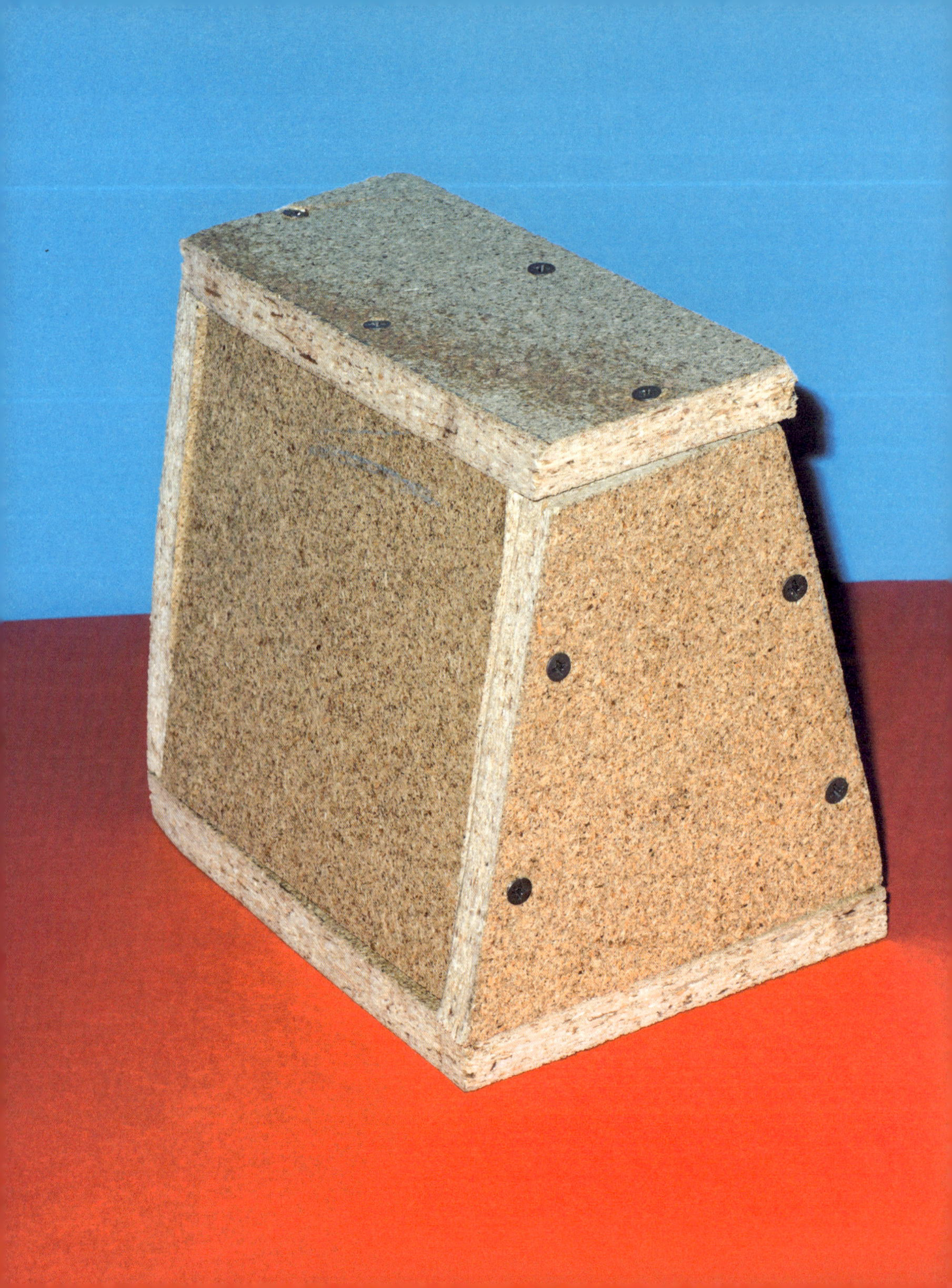

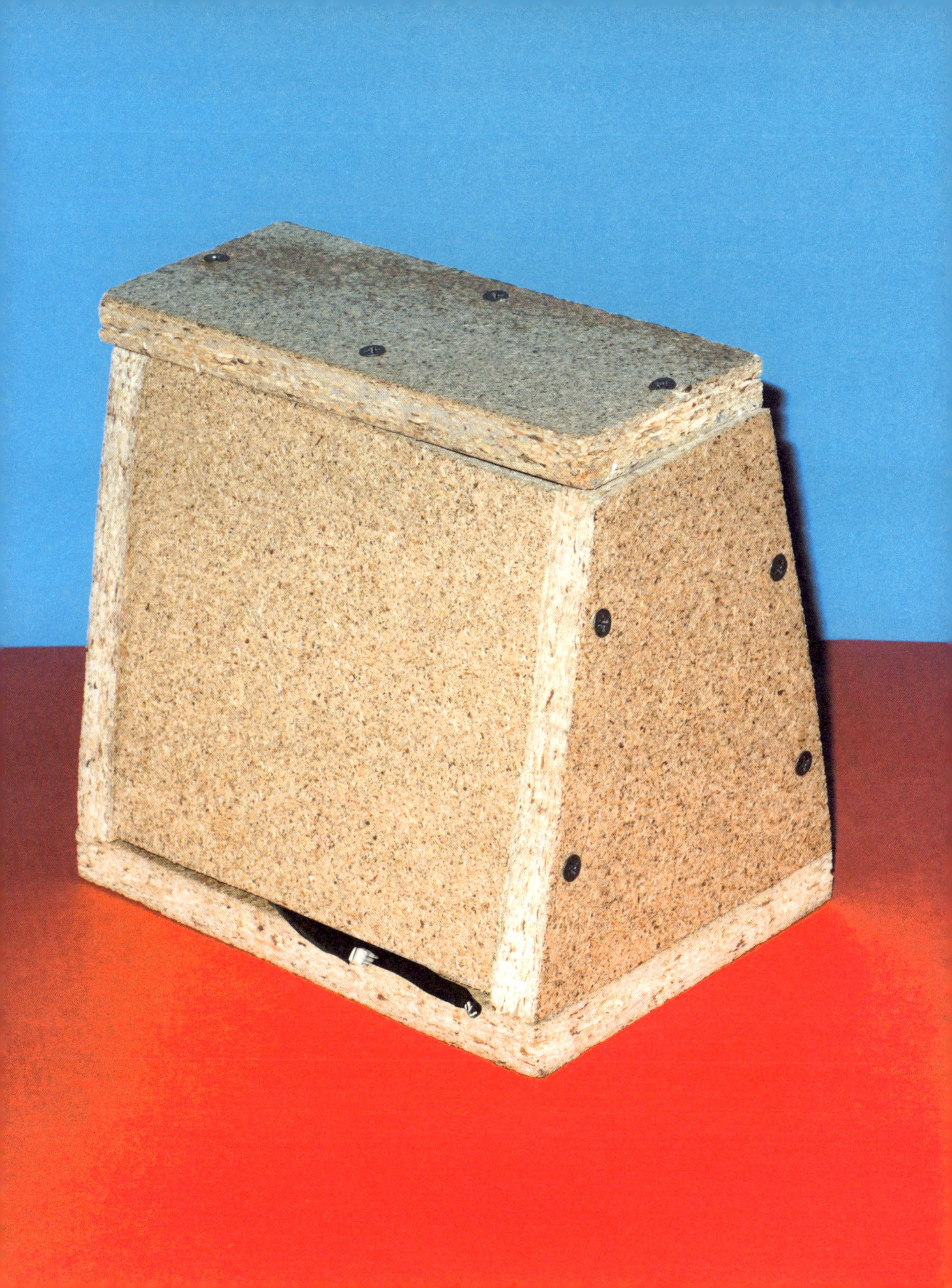

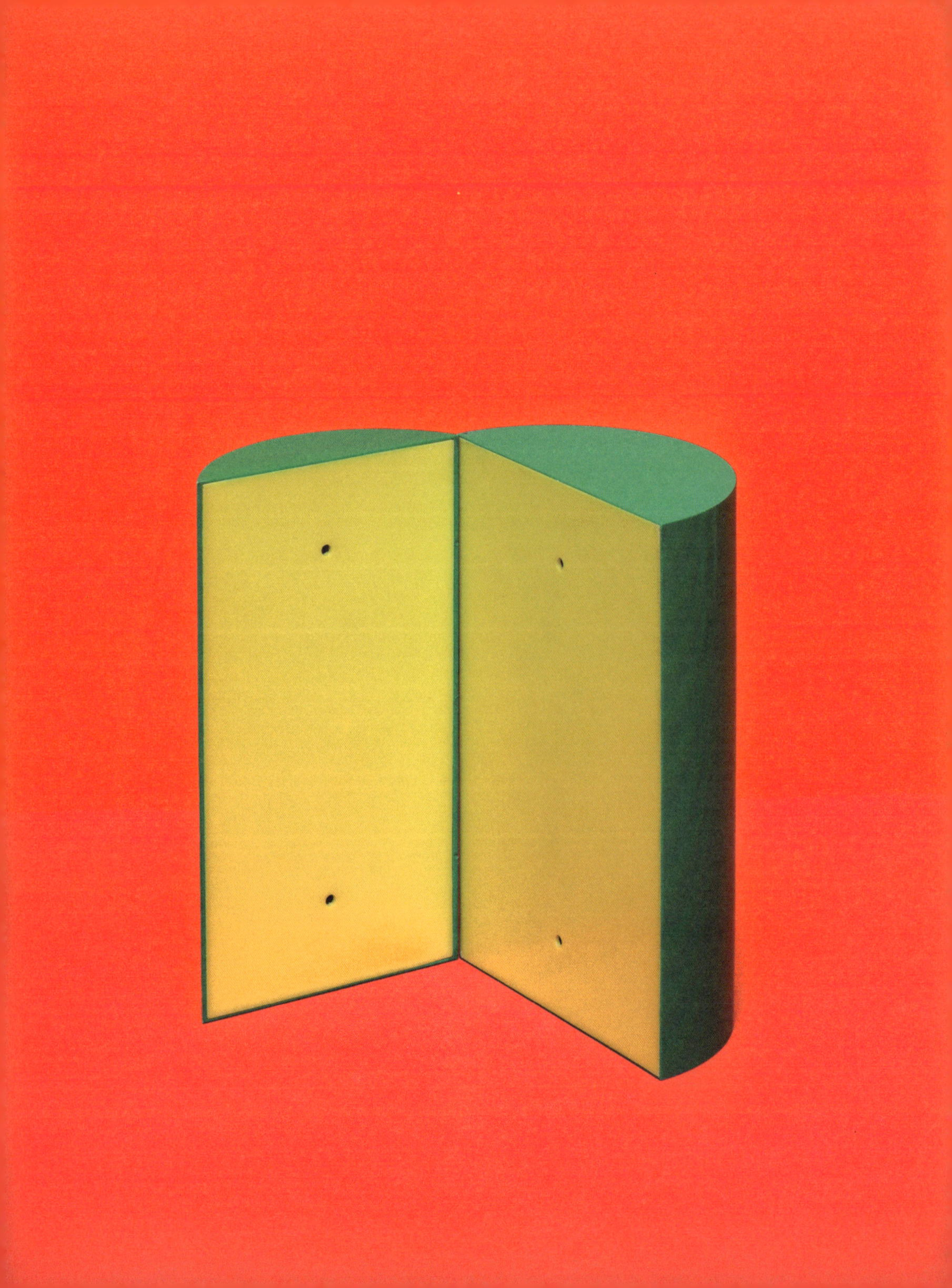

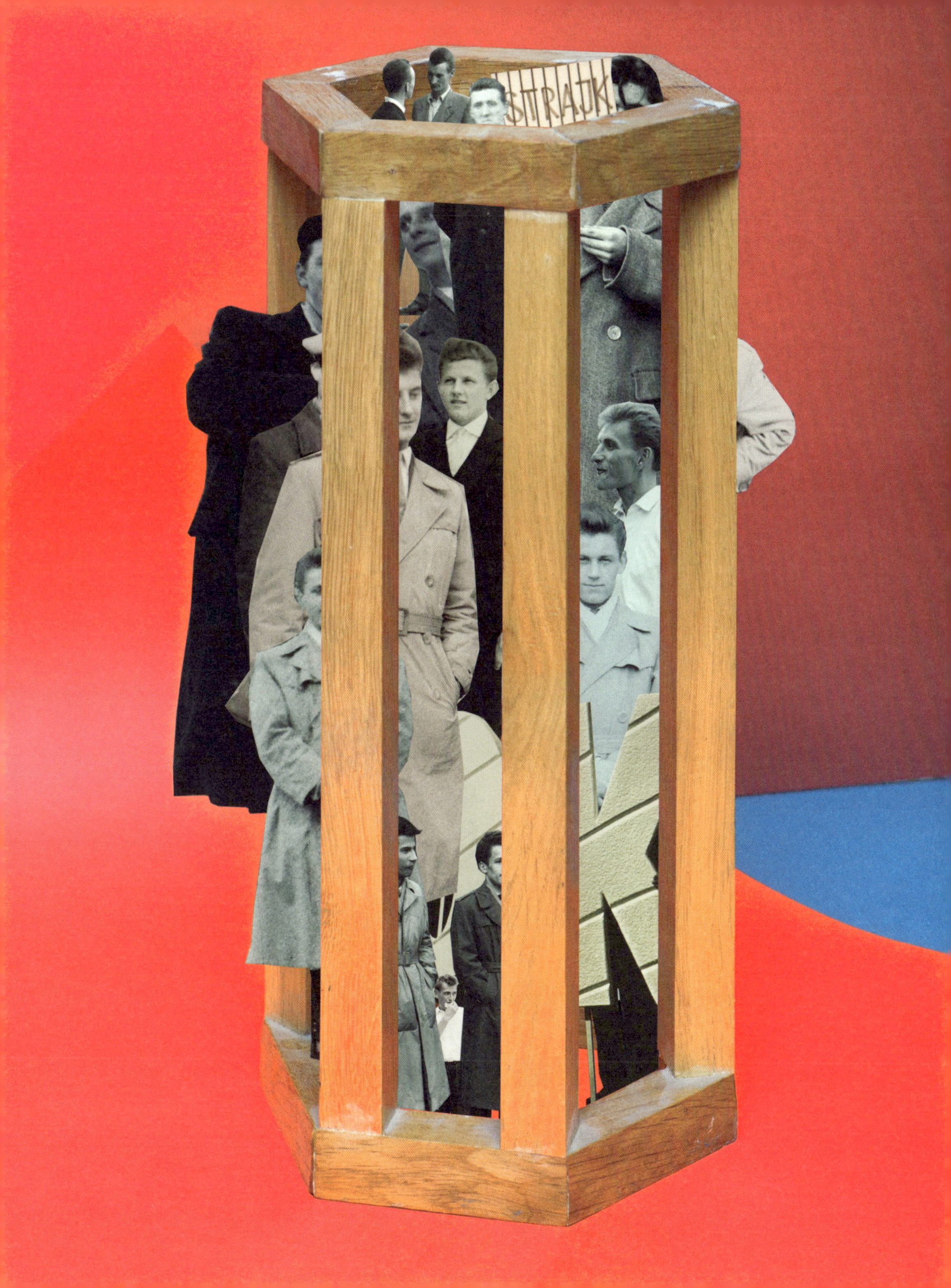
STRAJK

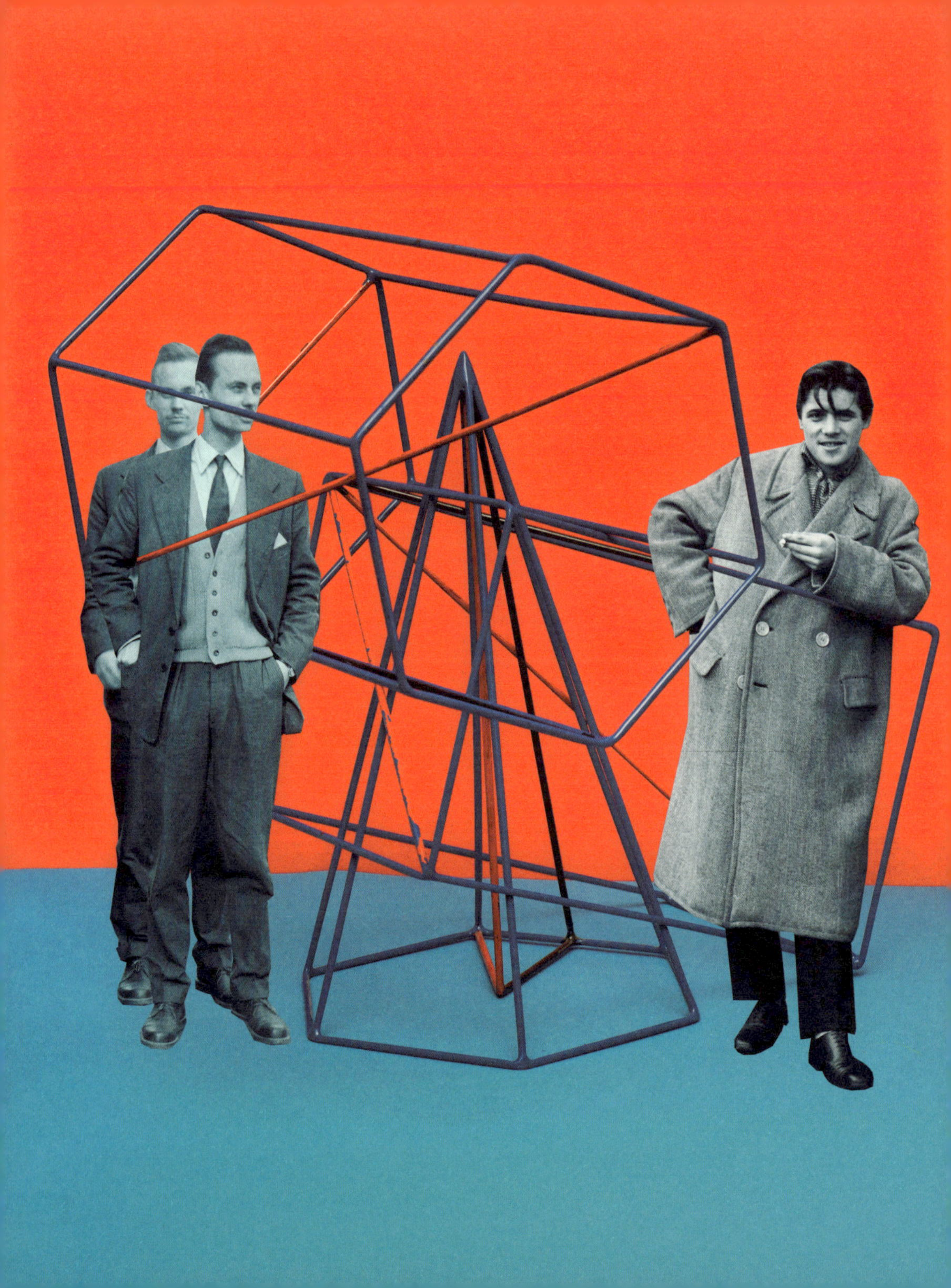

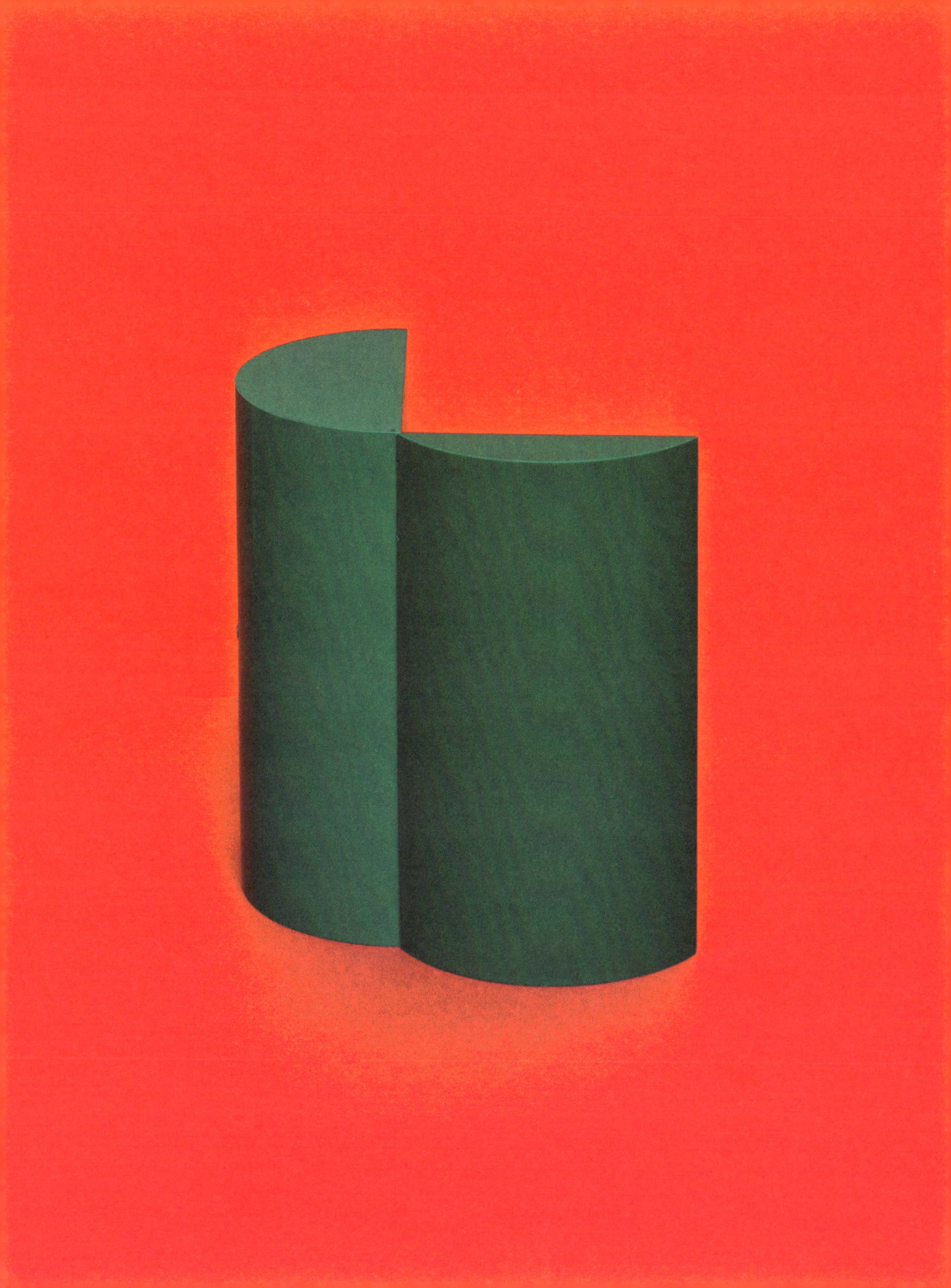

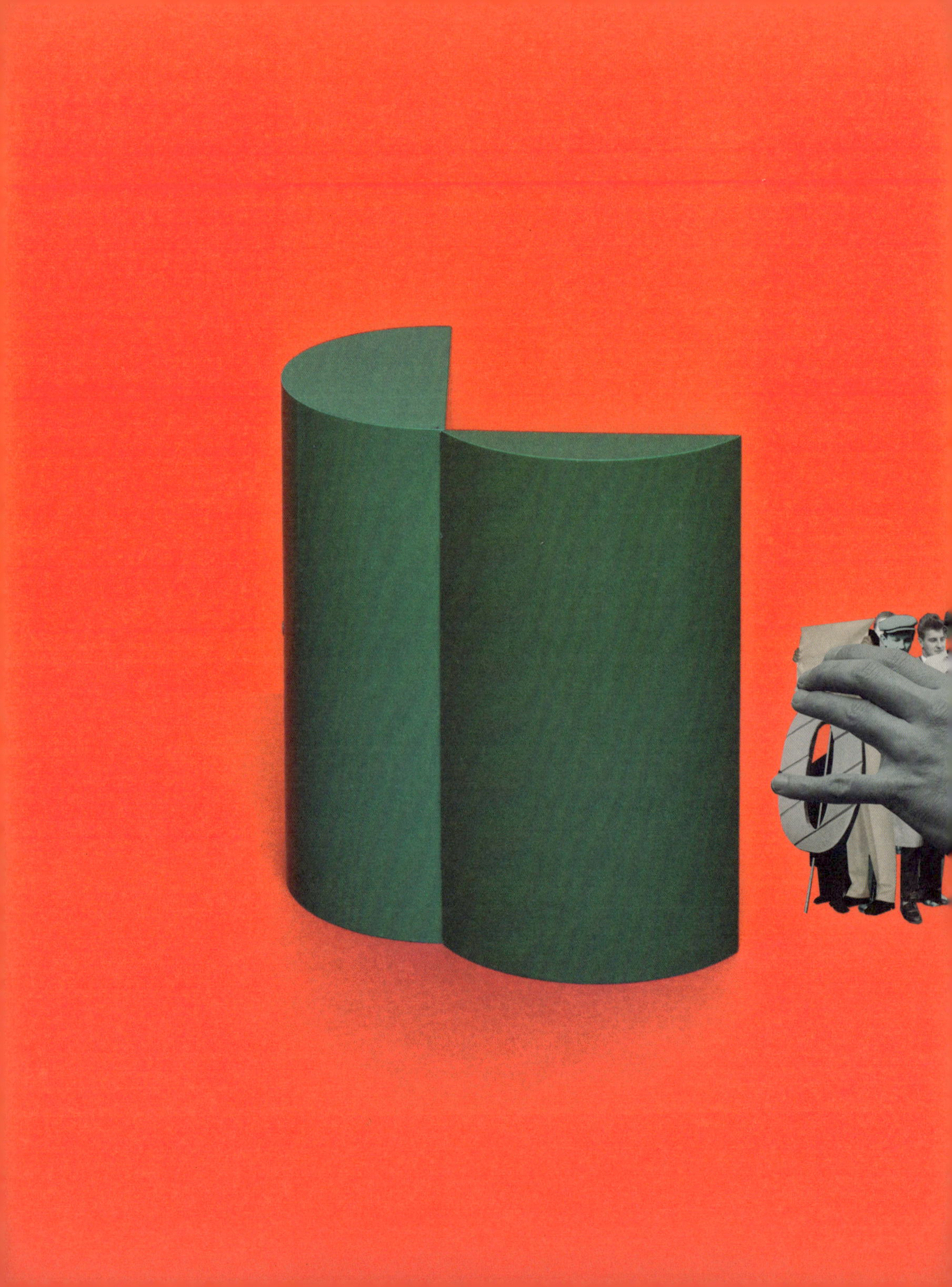

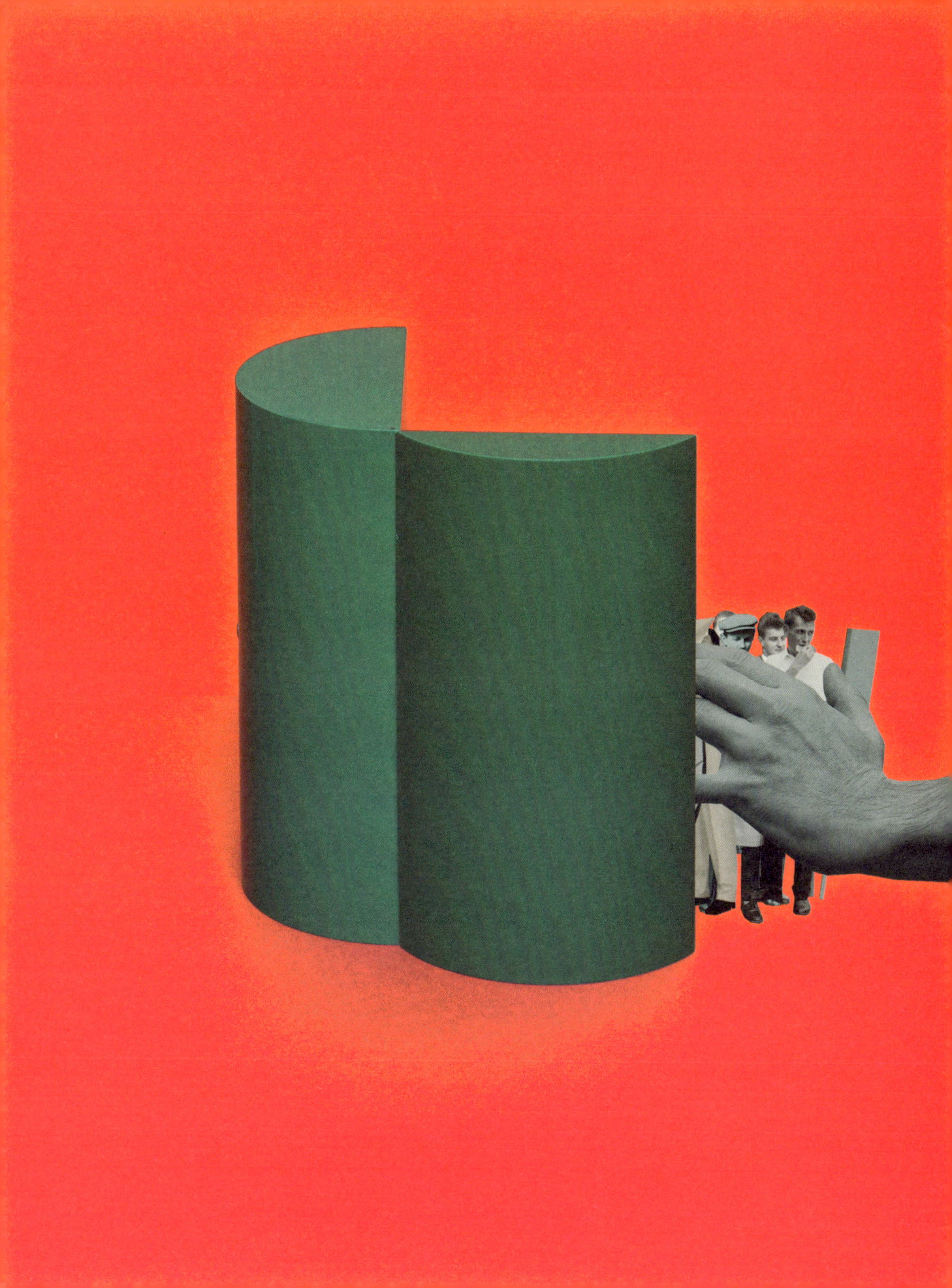

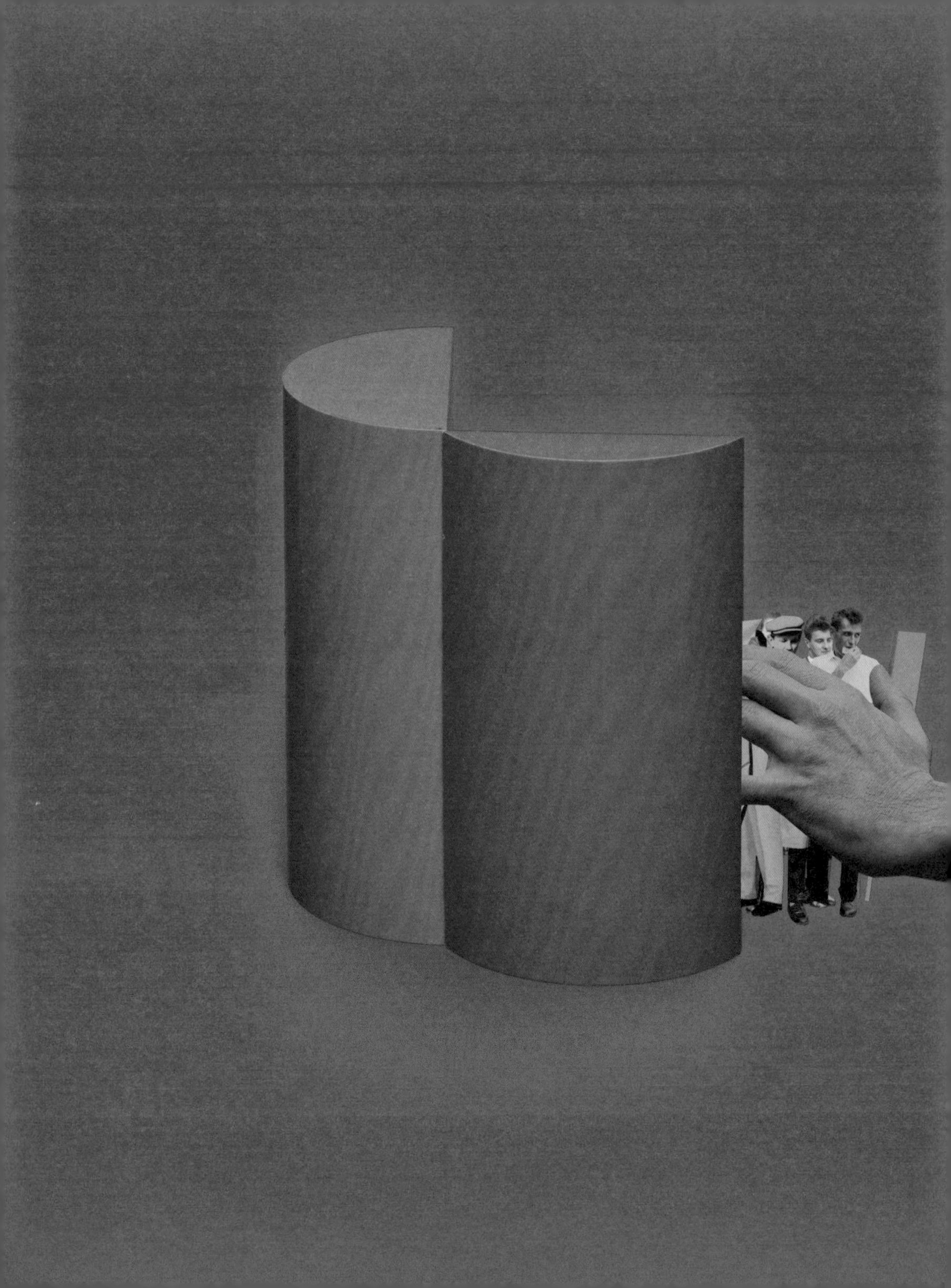

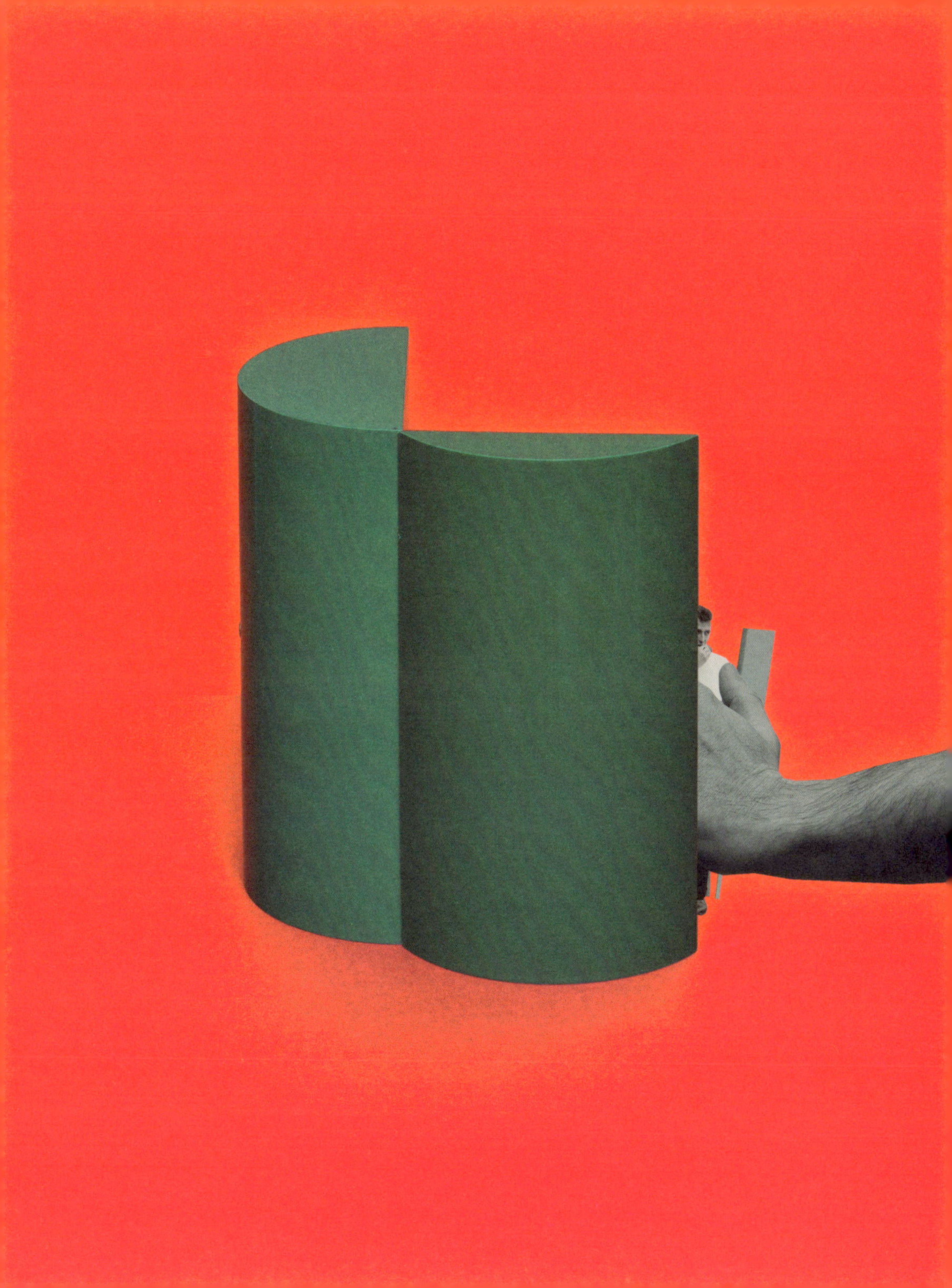

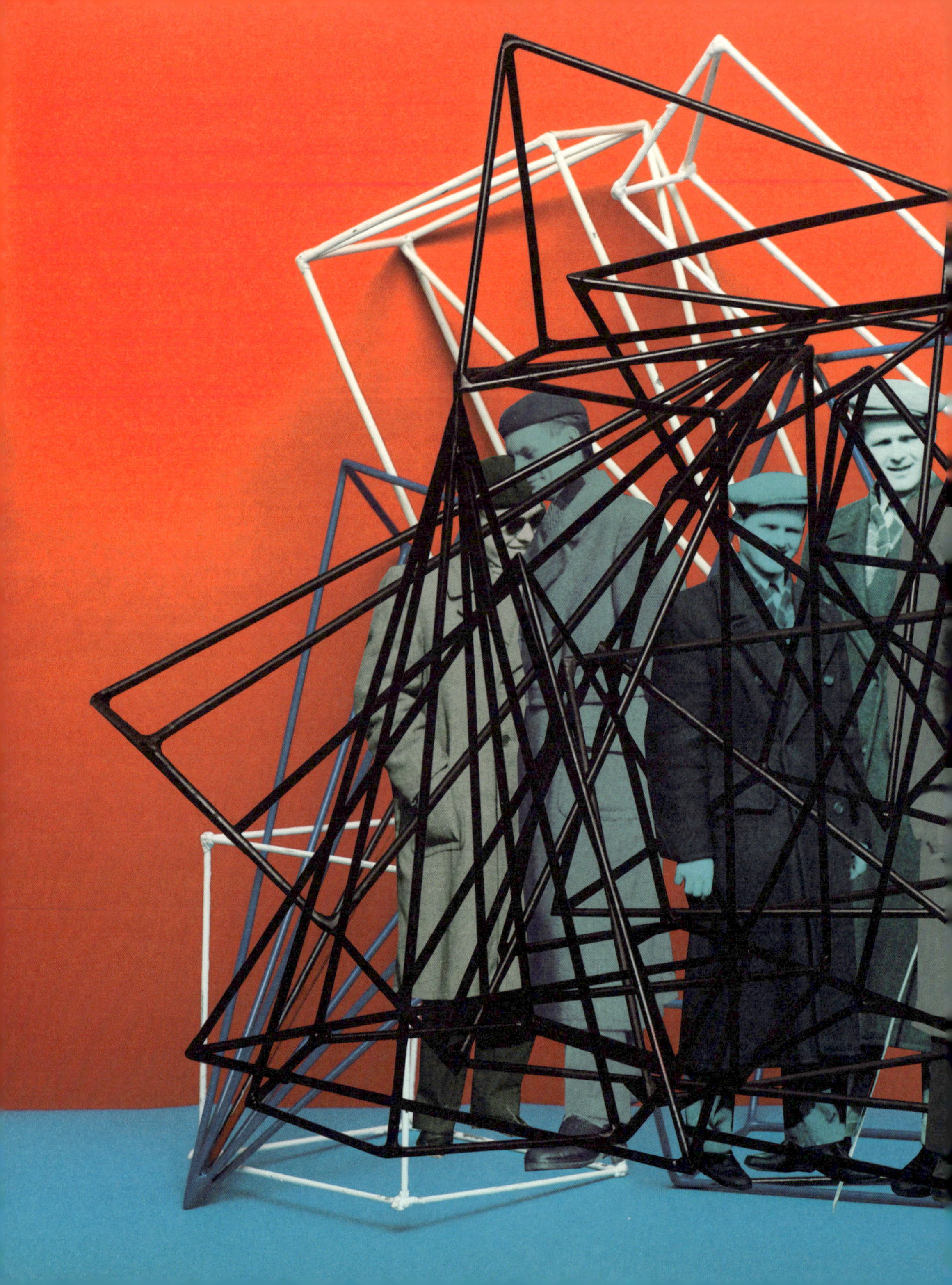

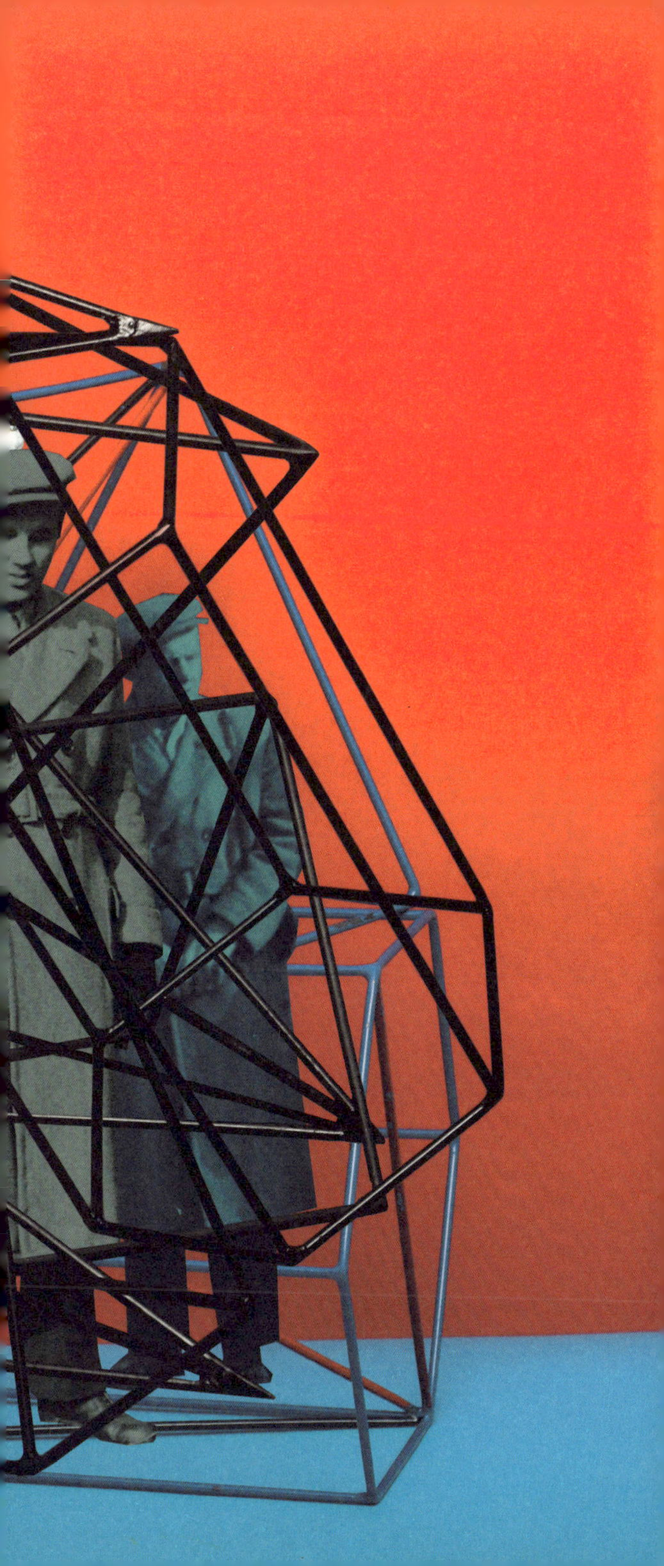

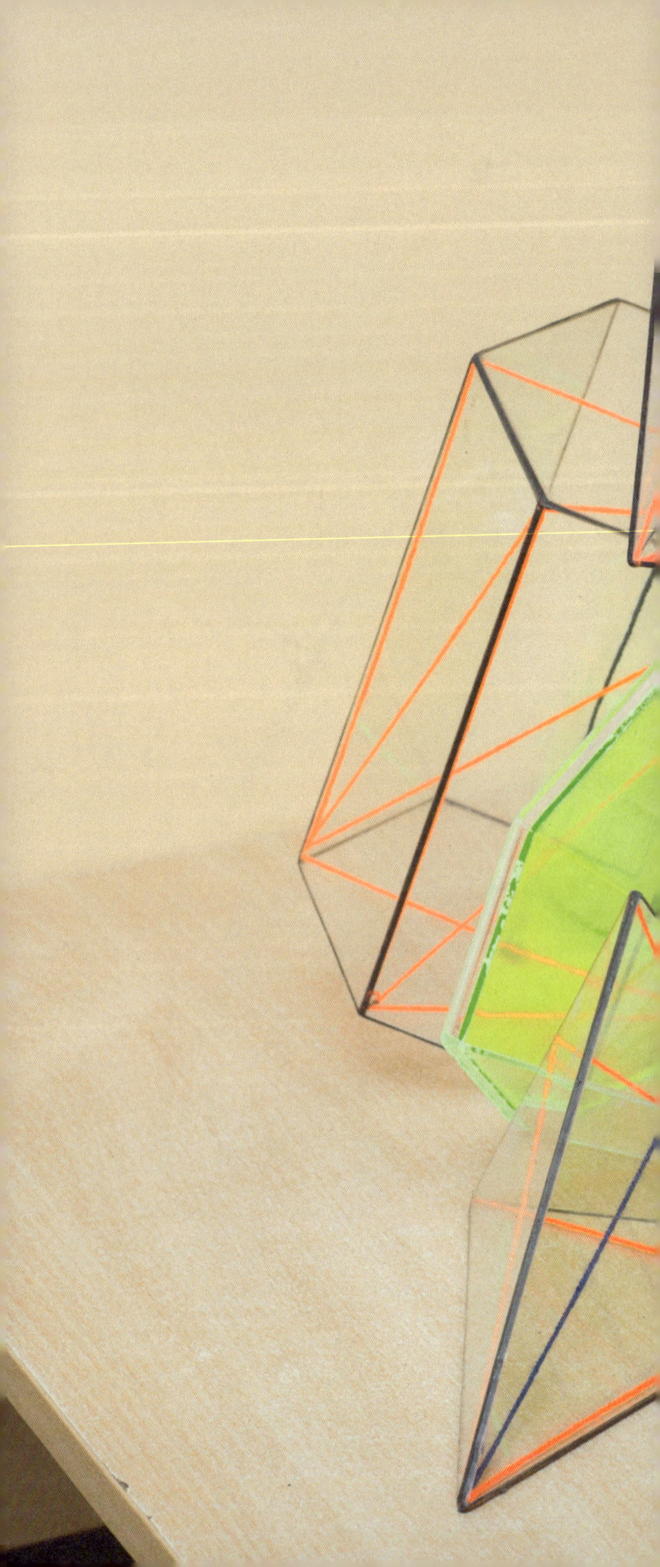

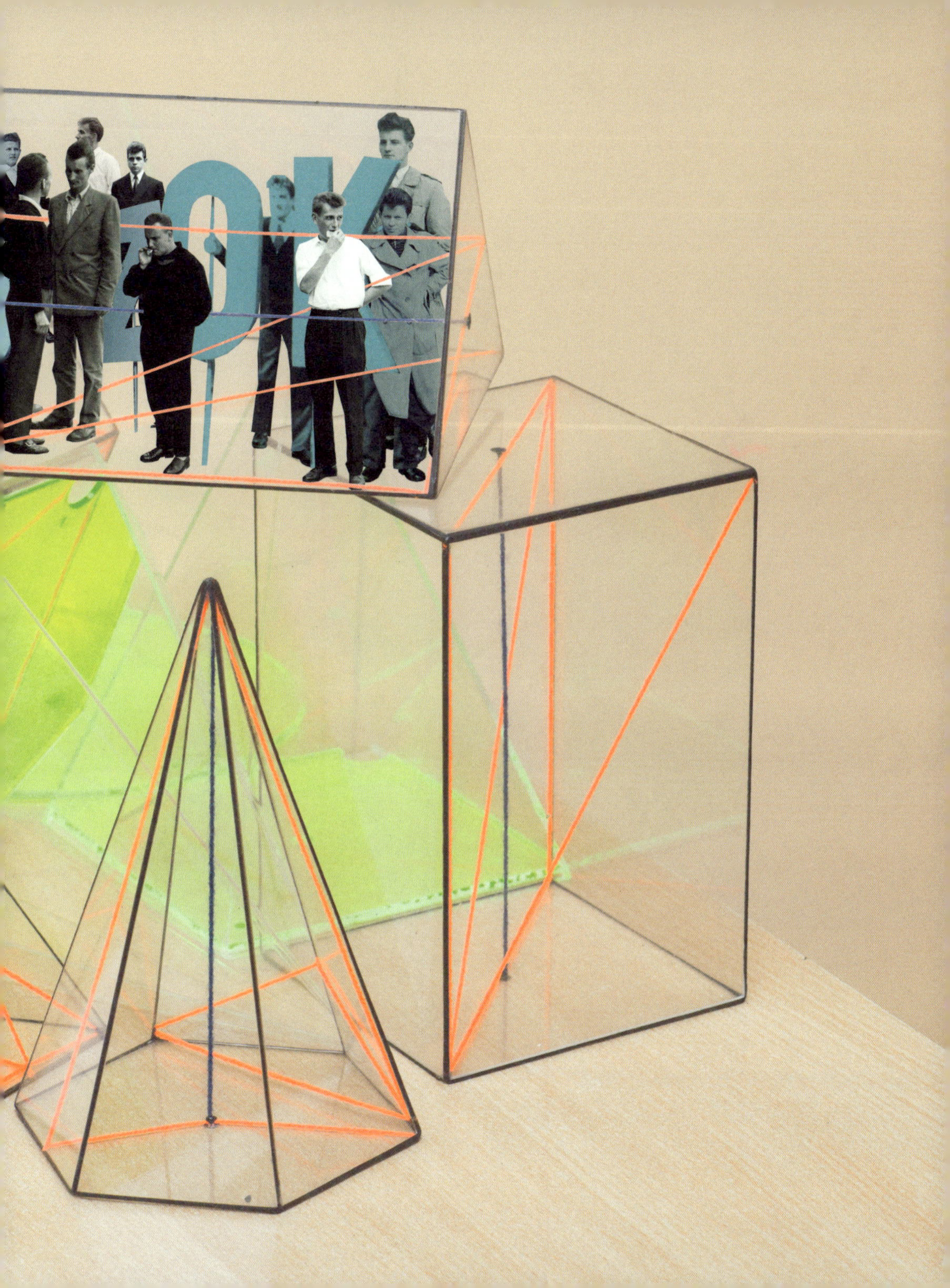

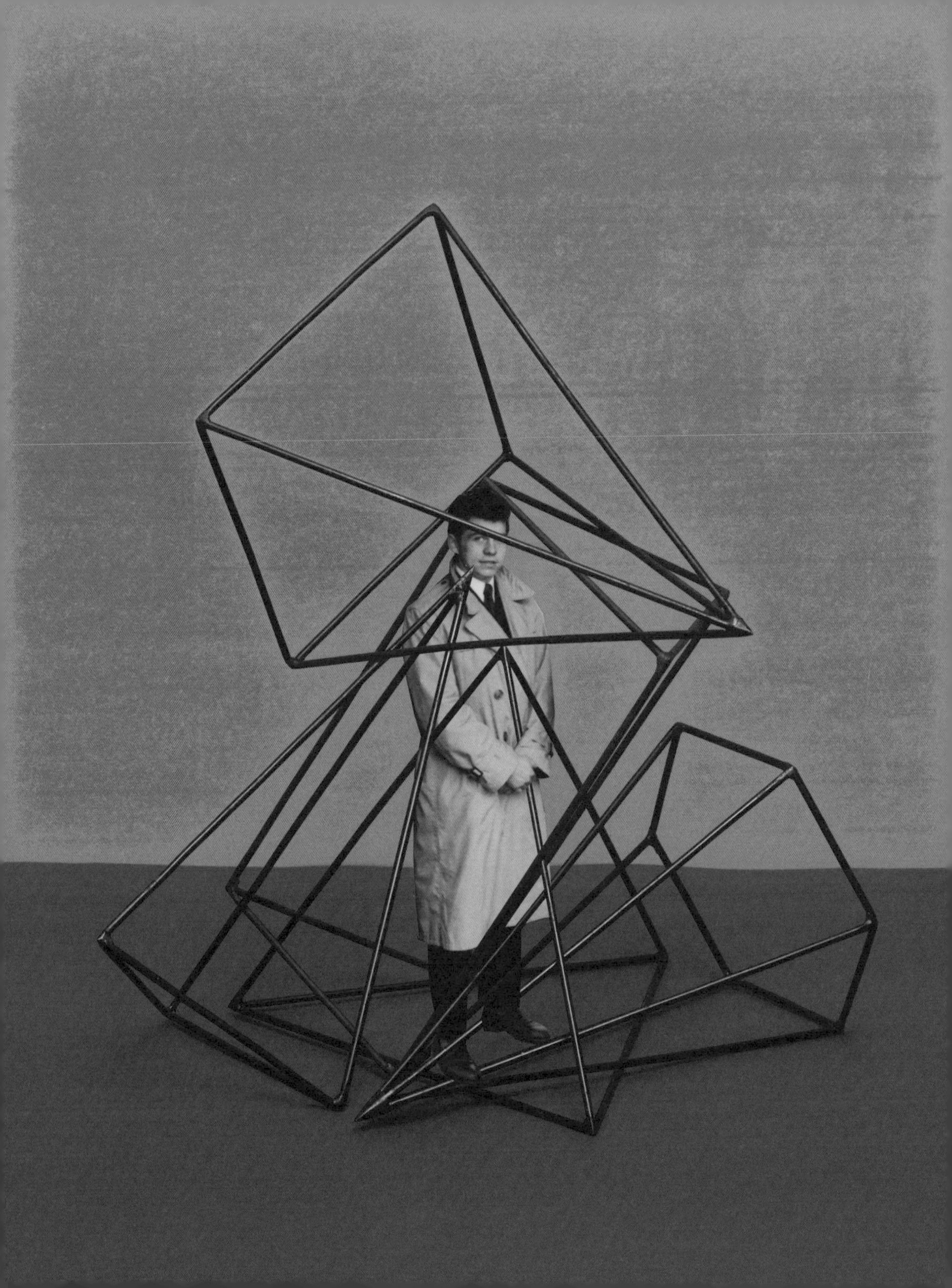

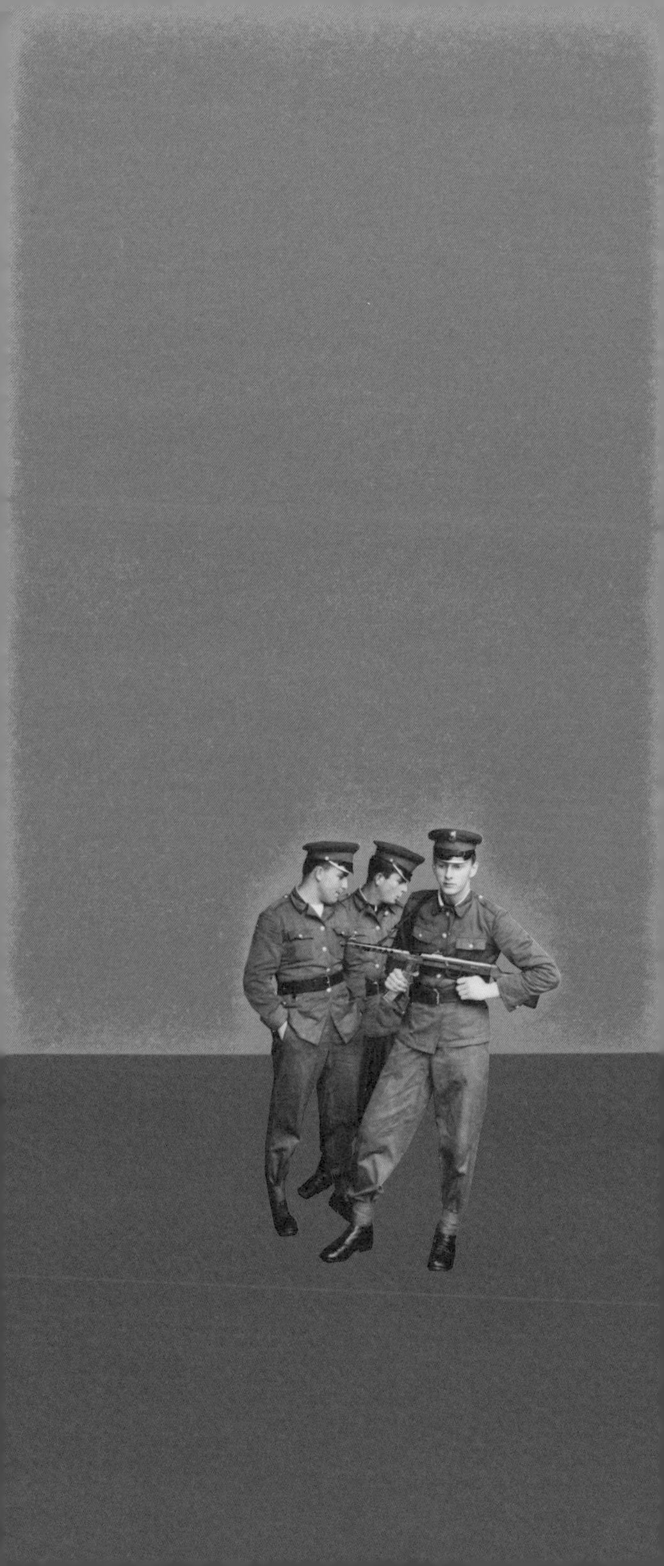

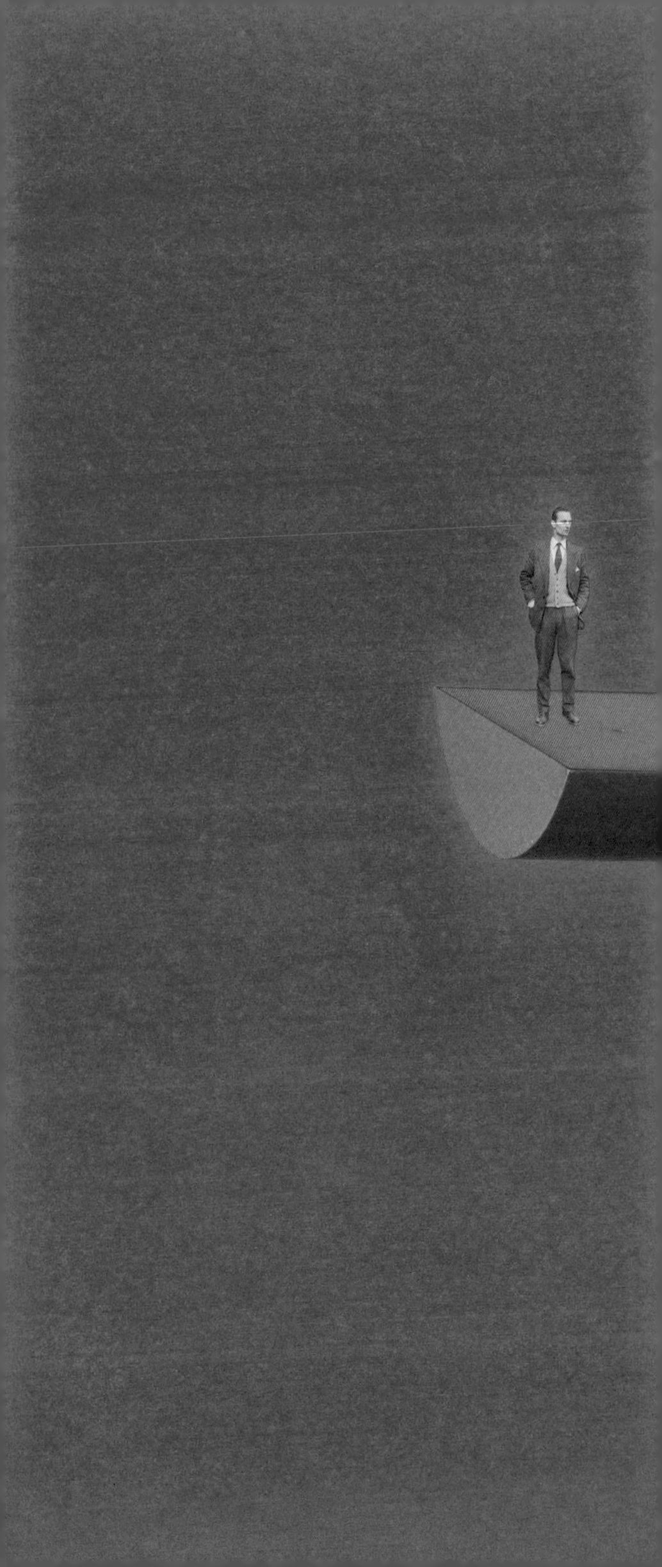

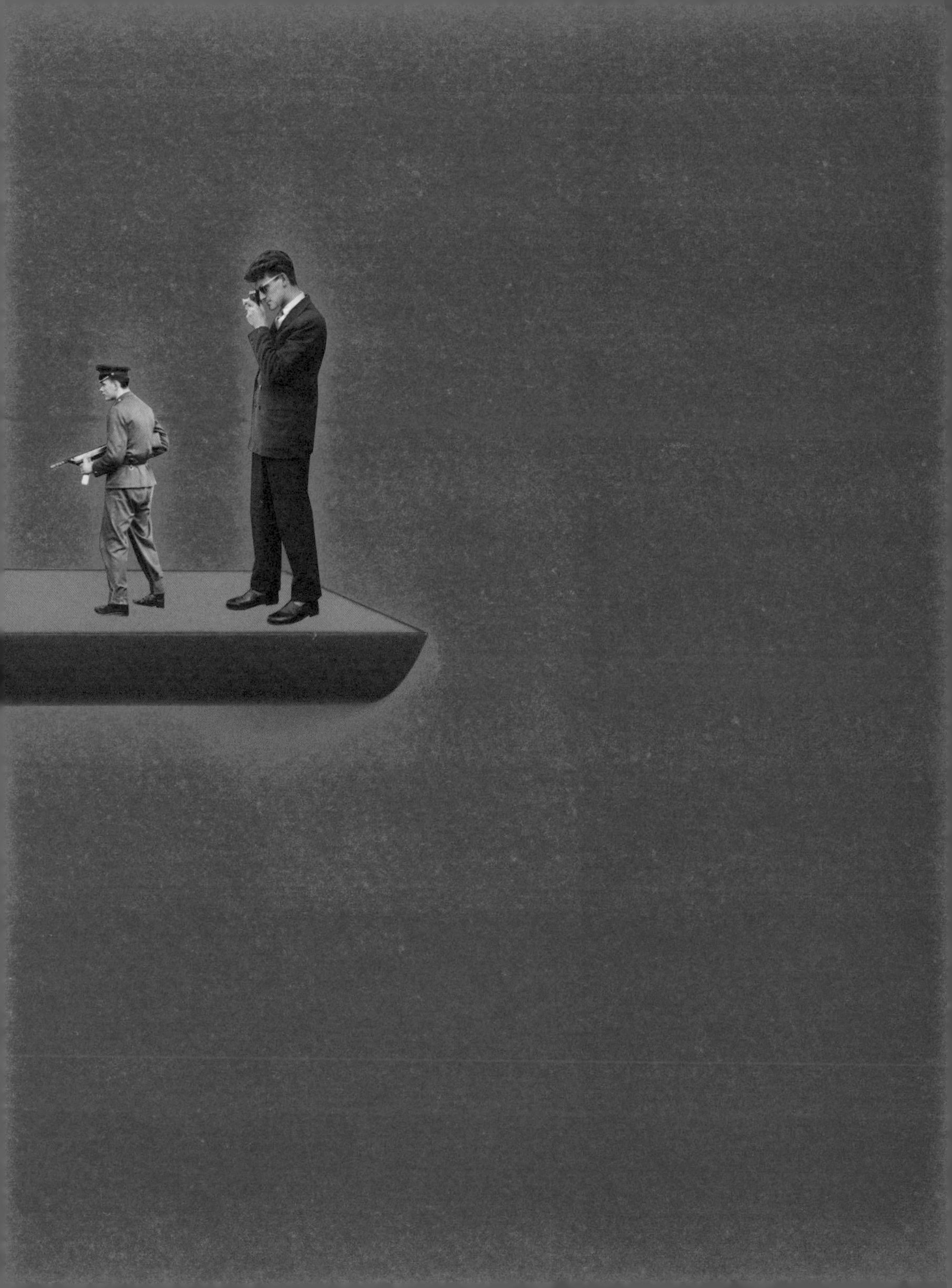

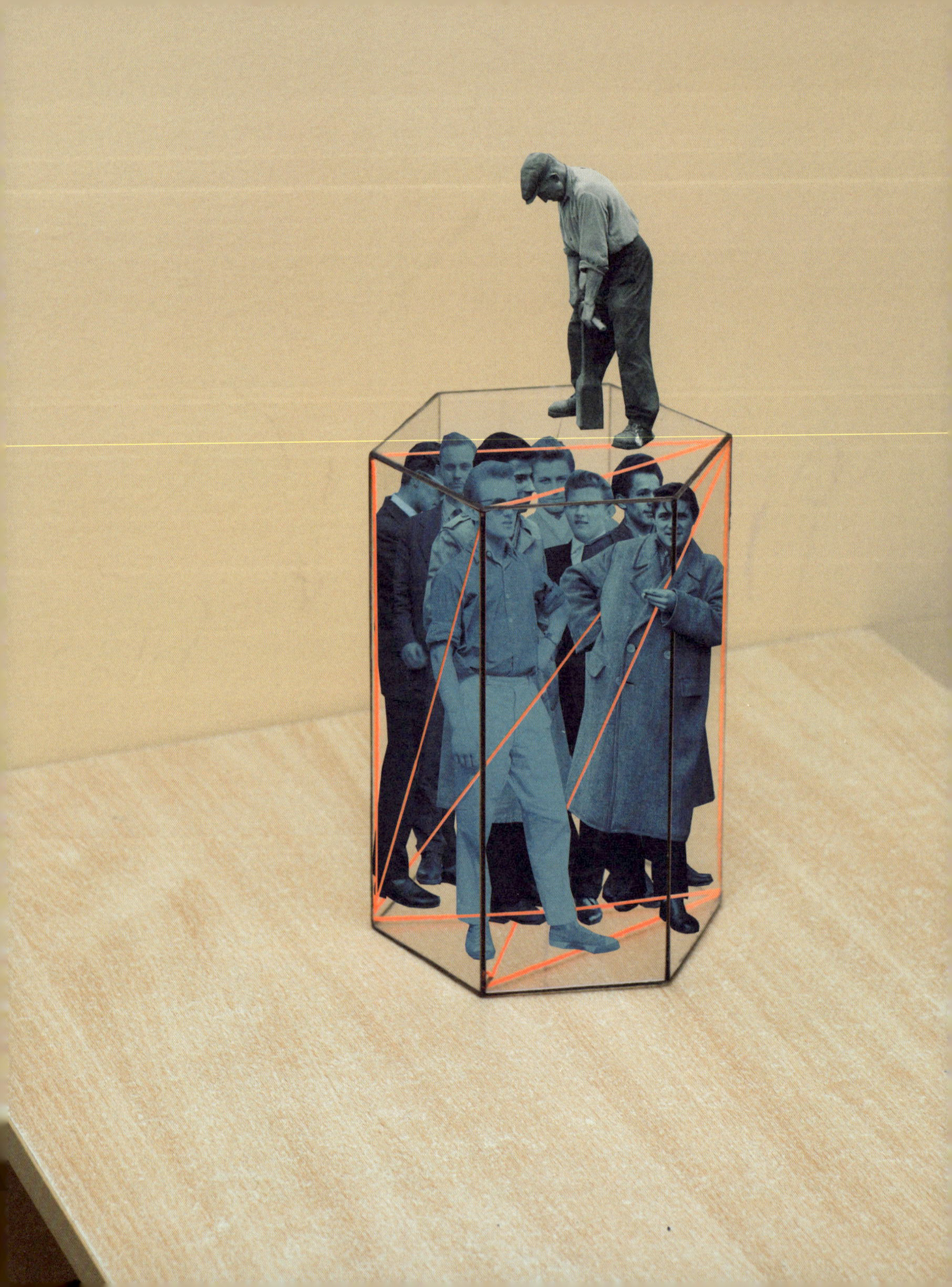

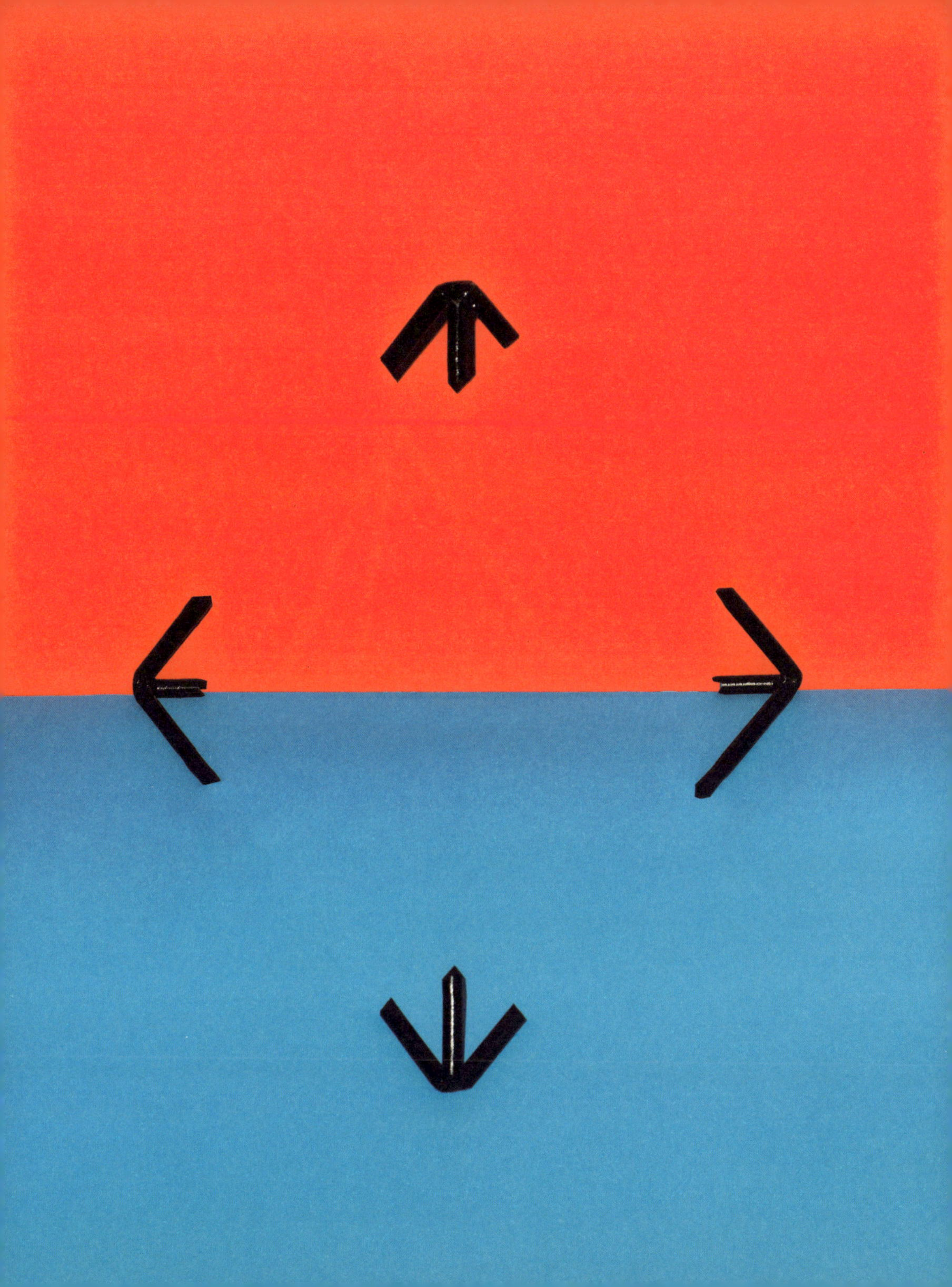

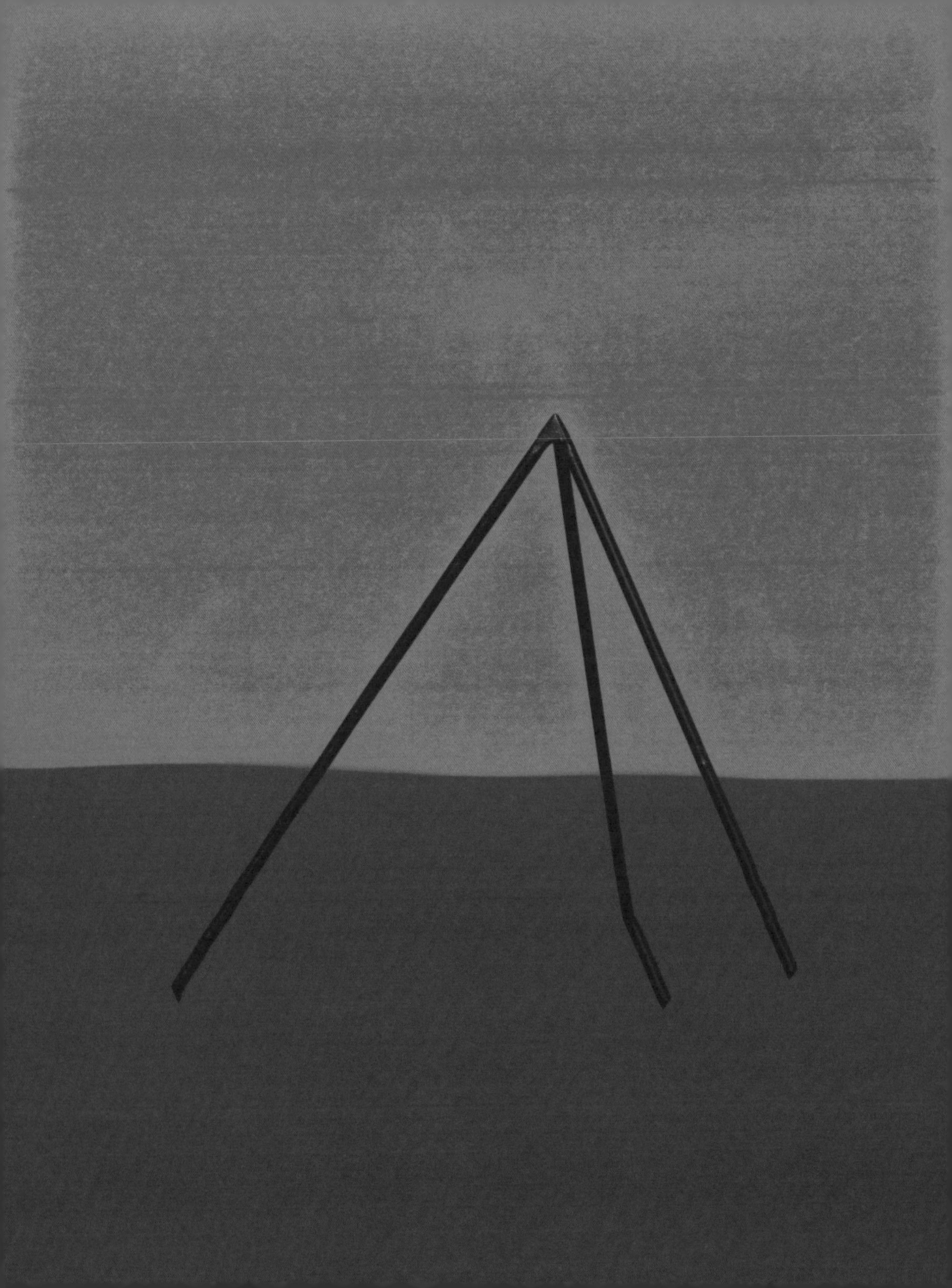

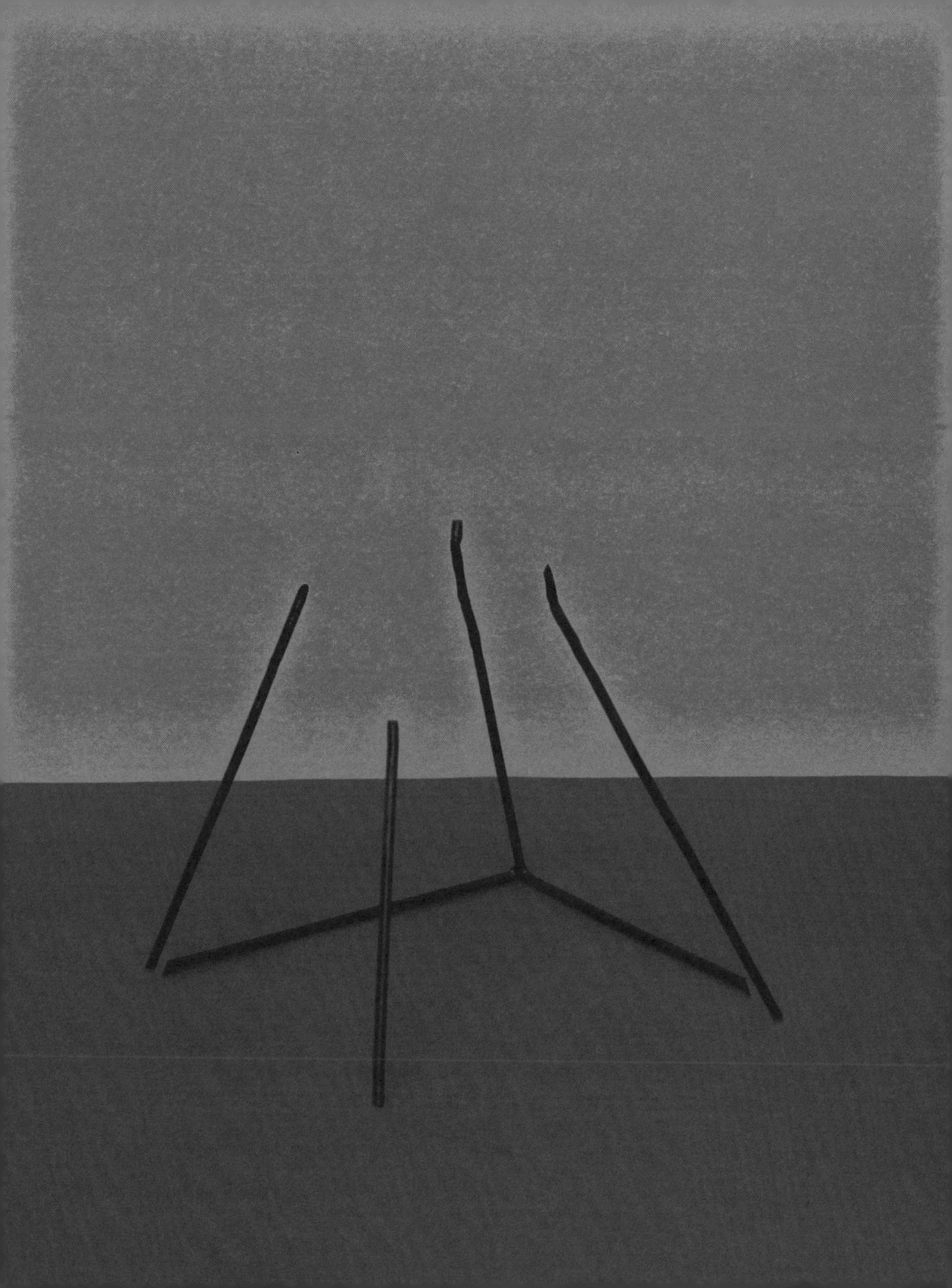

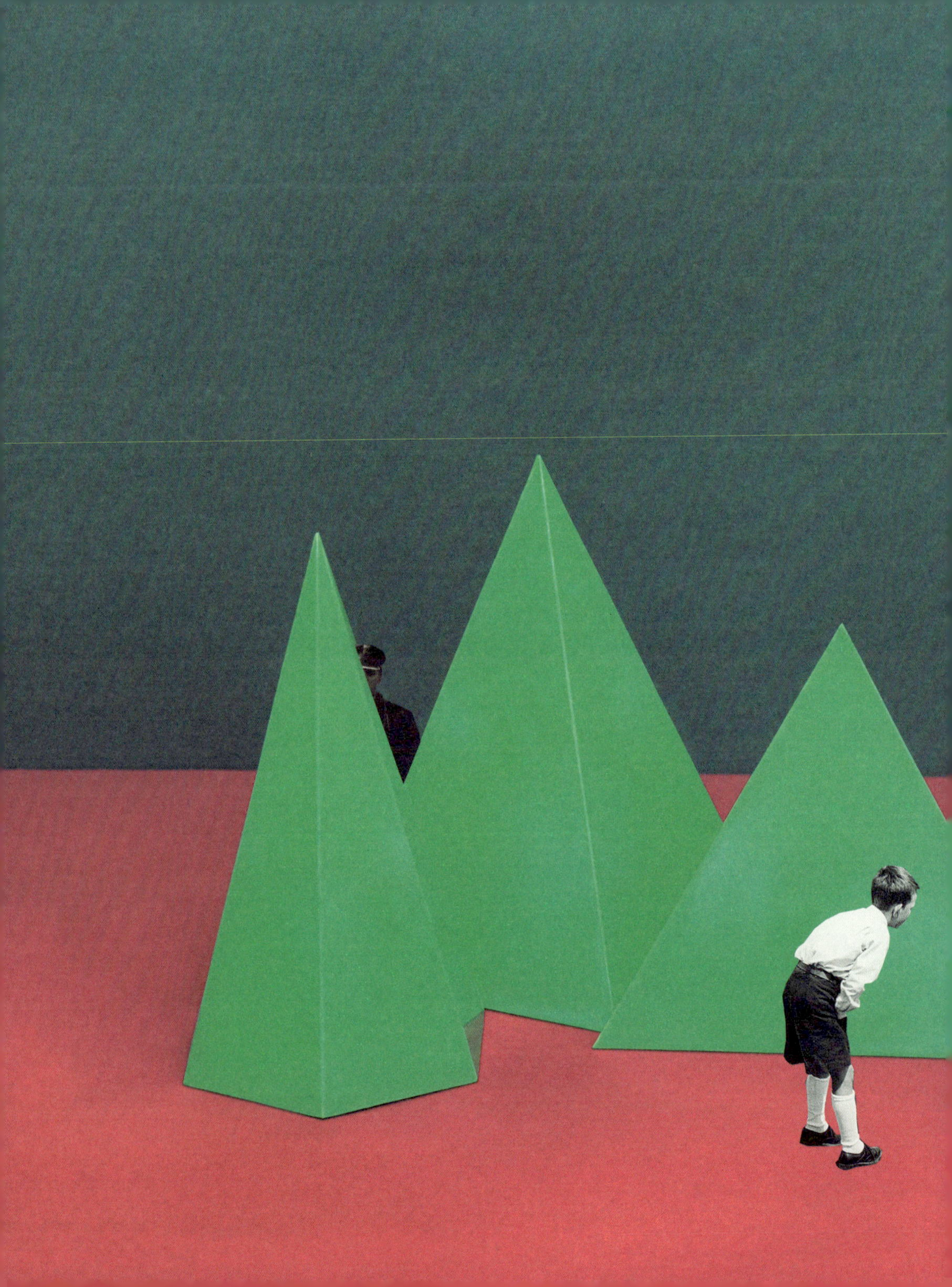

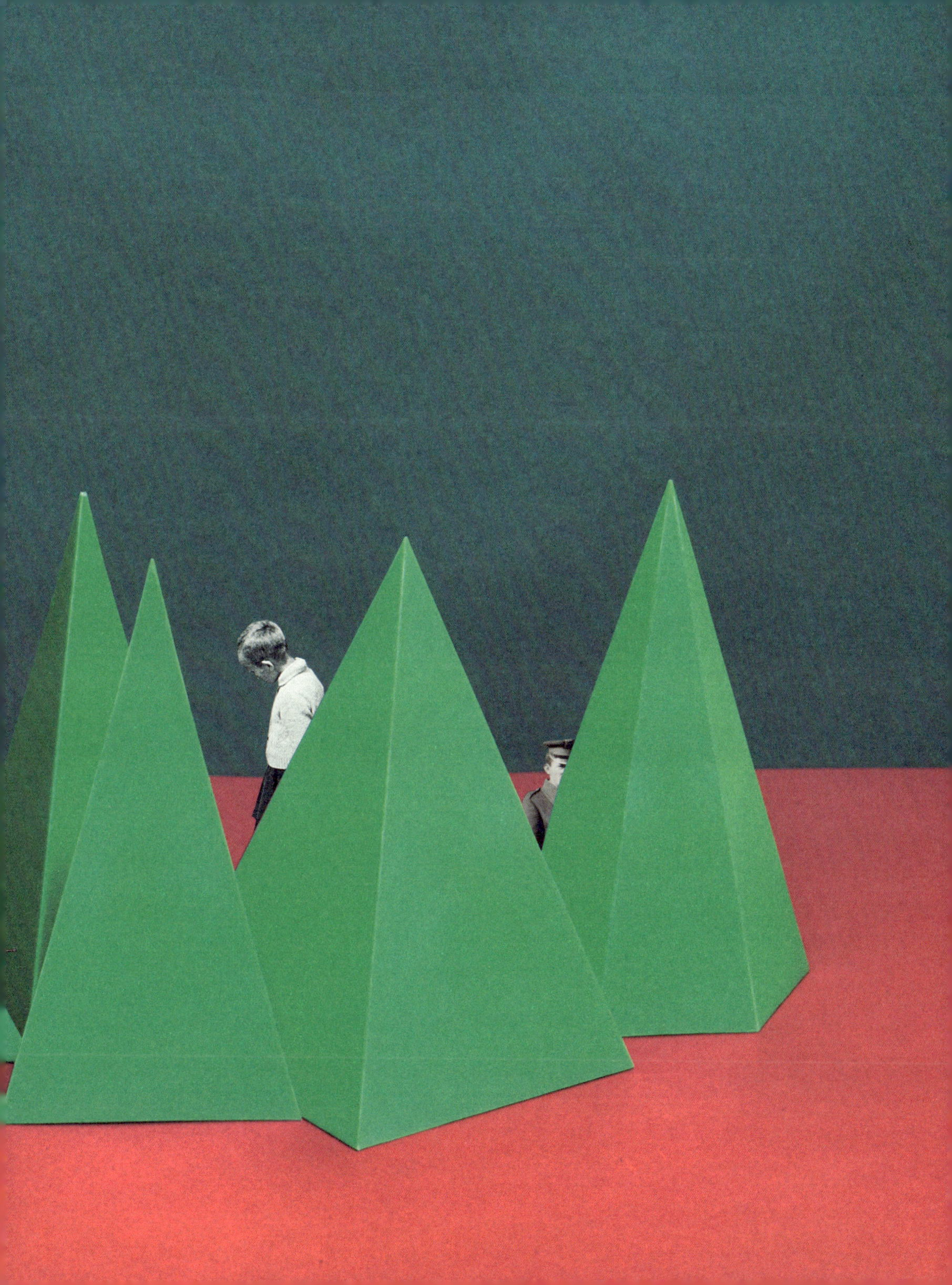

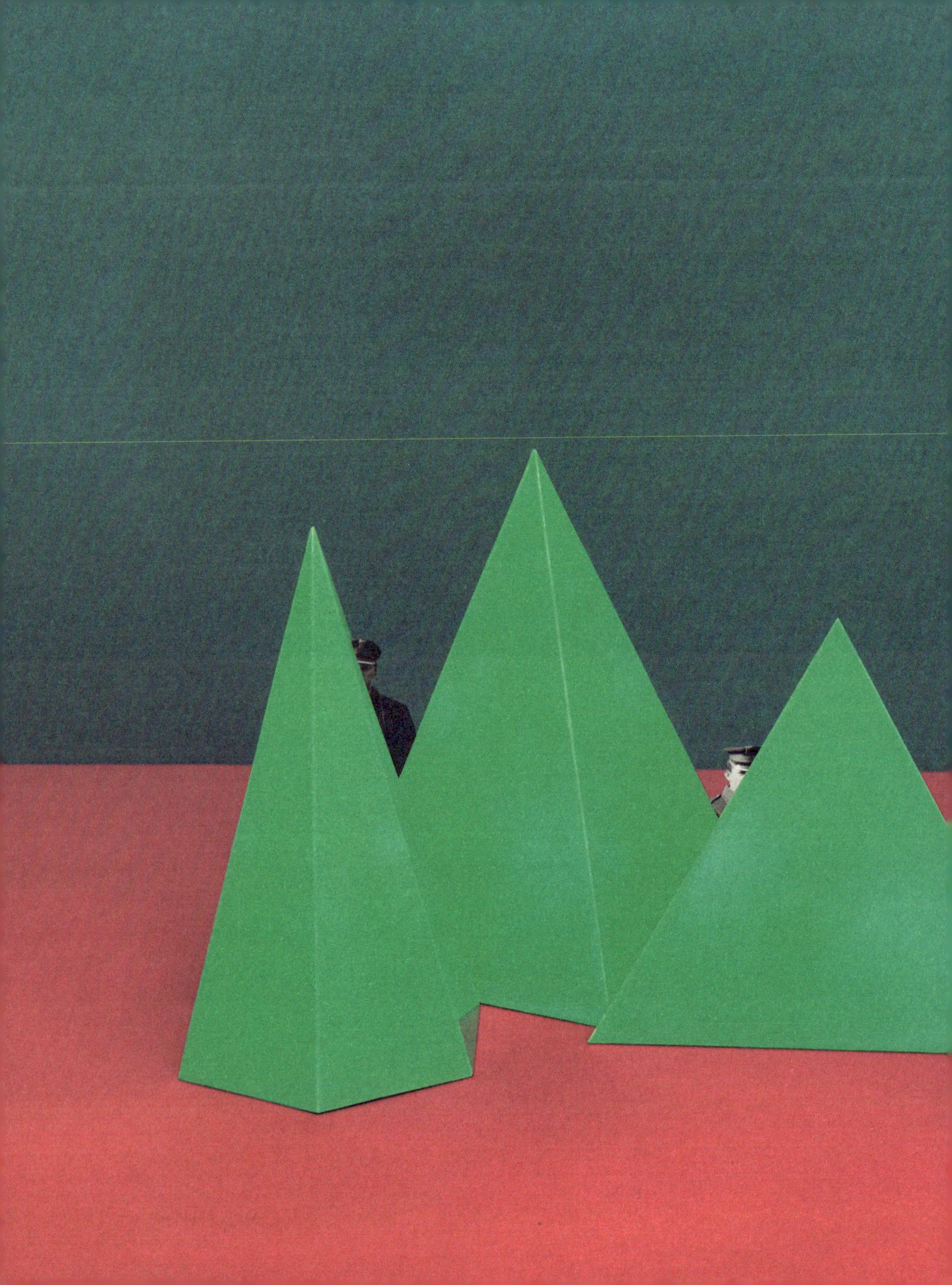

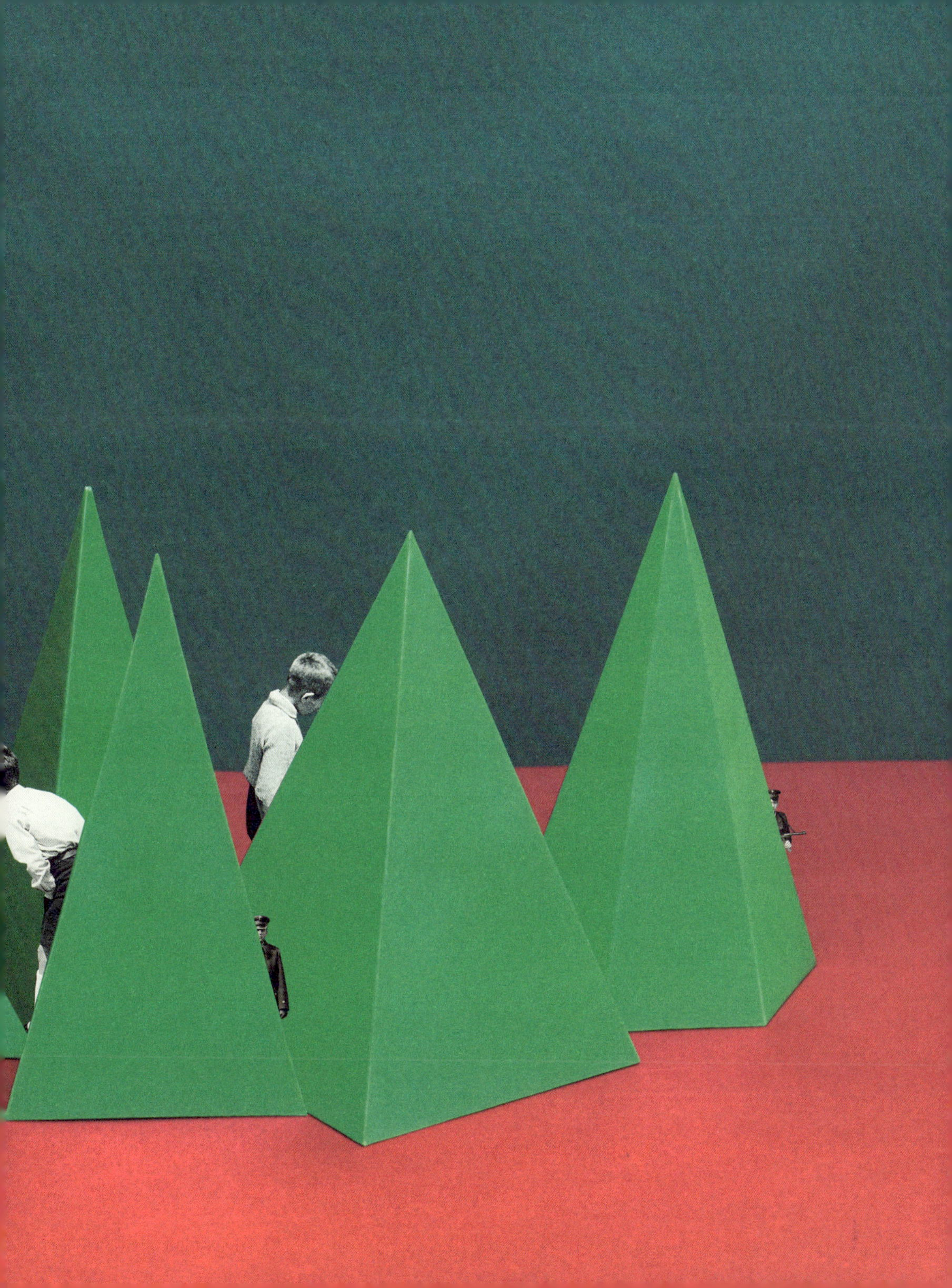

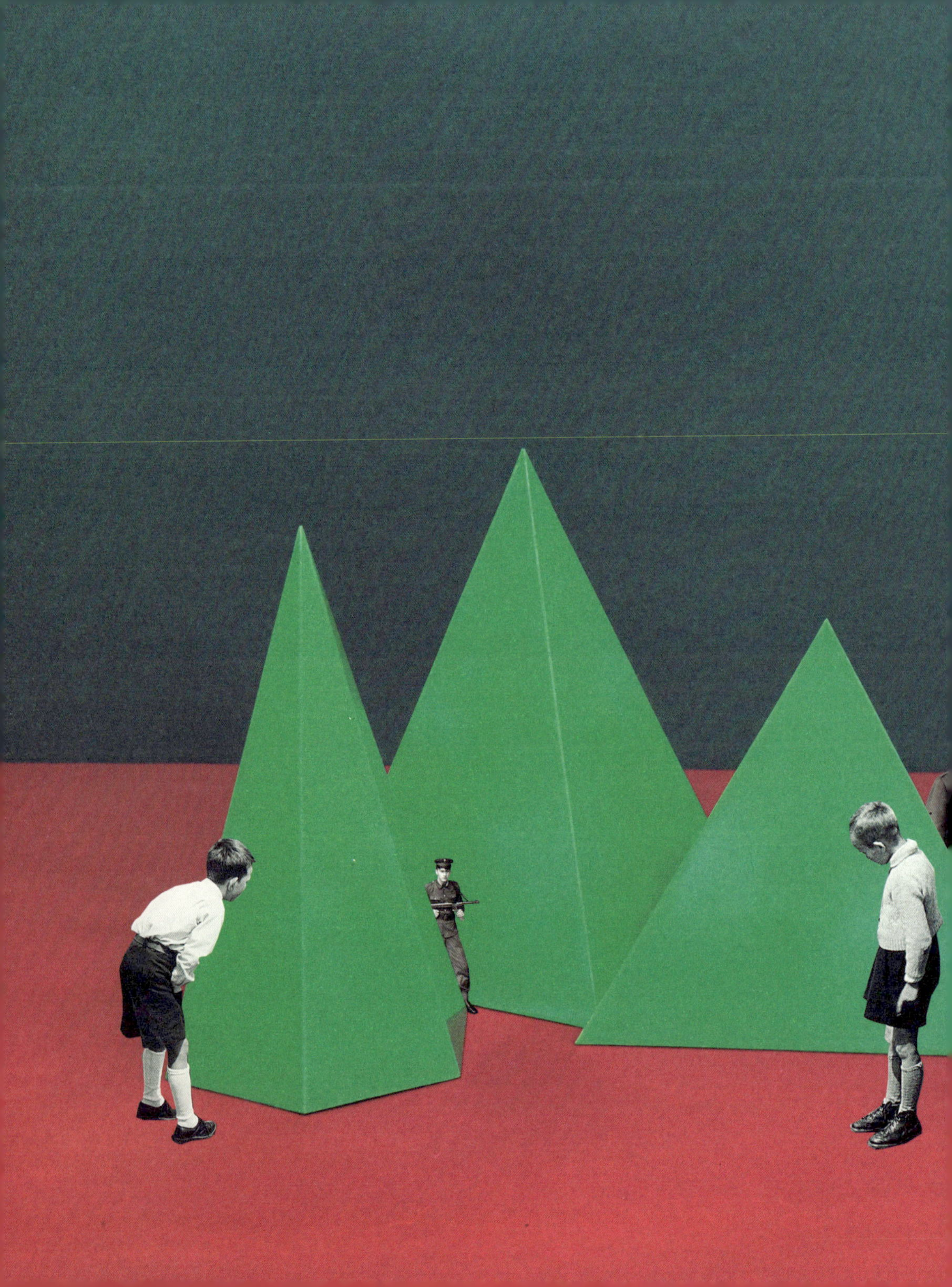

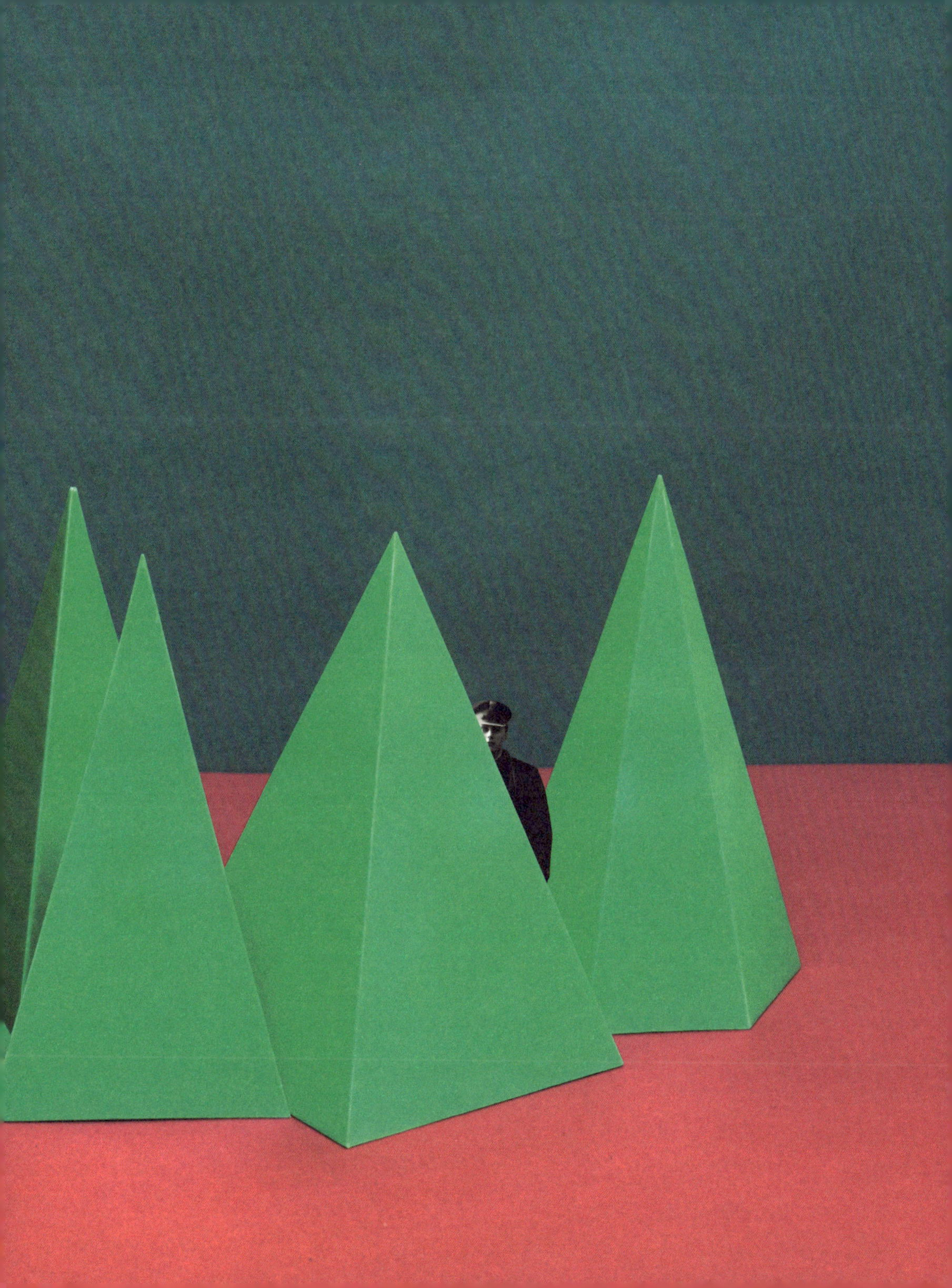

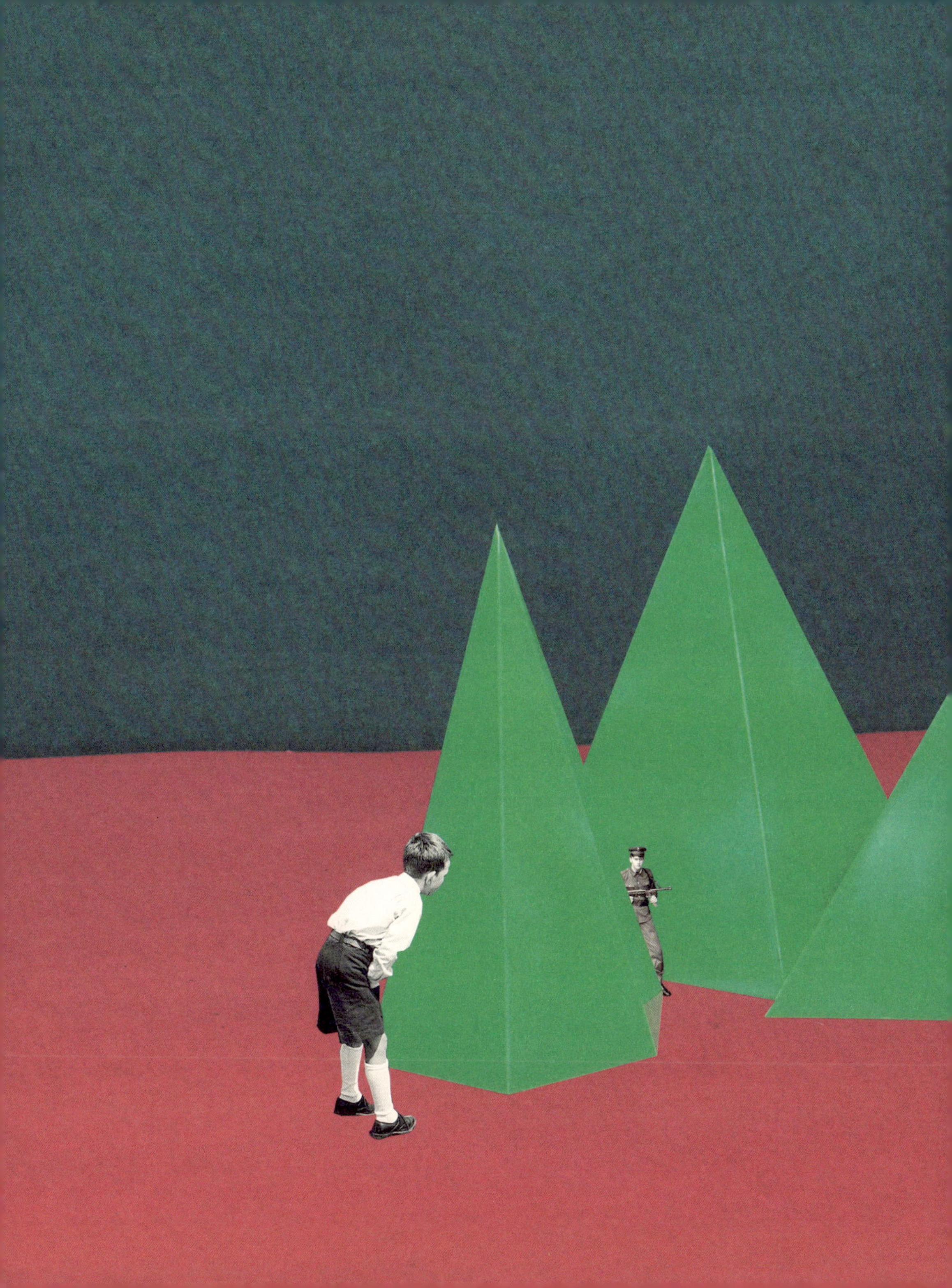

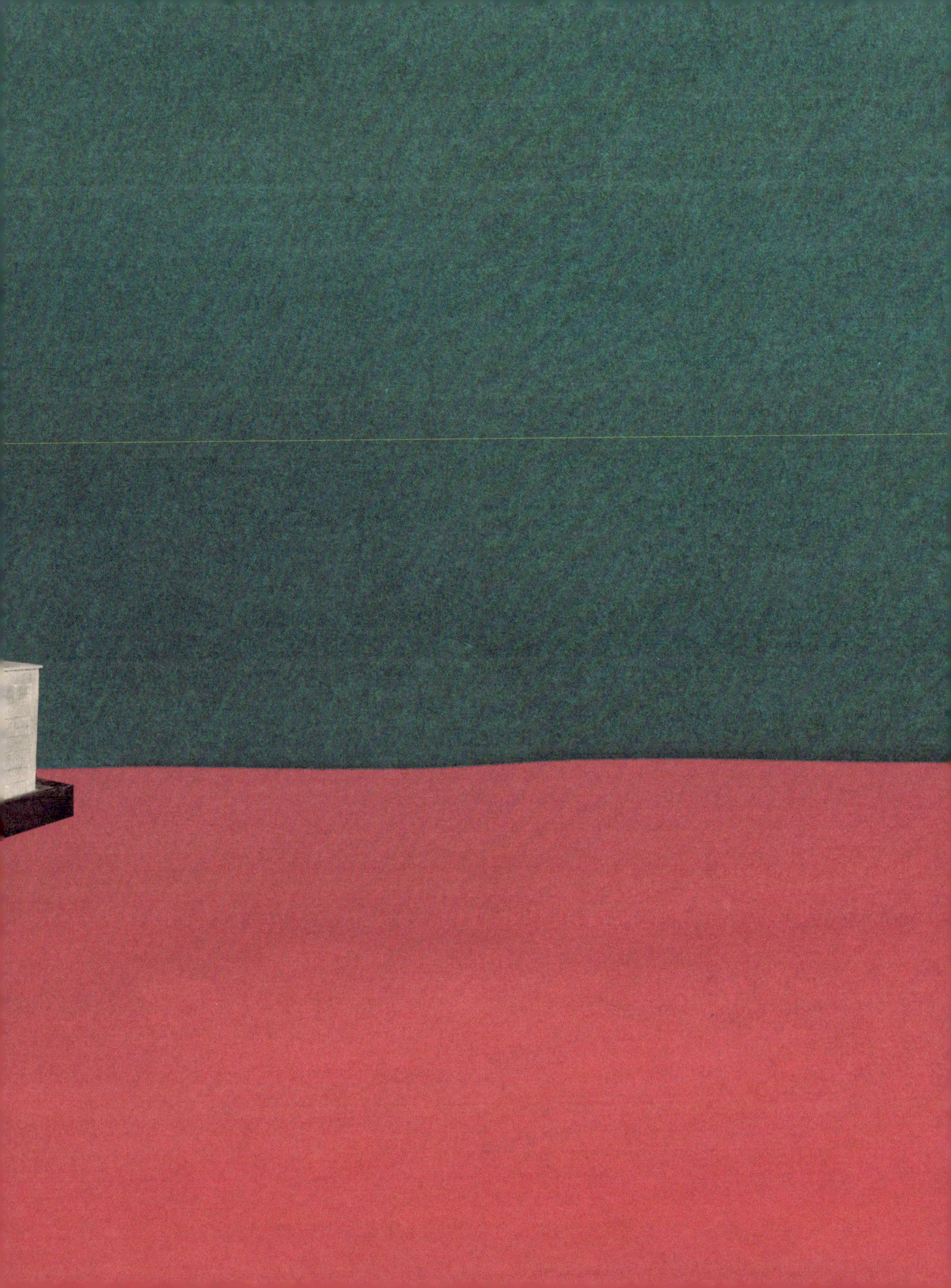

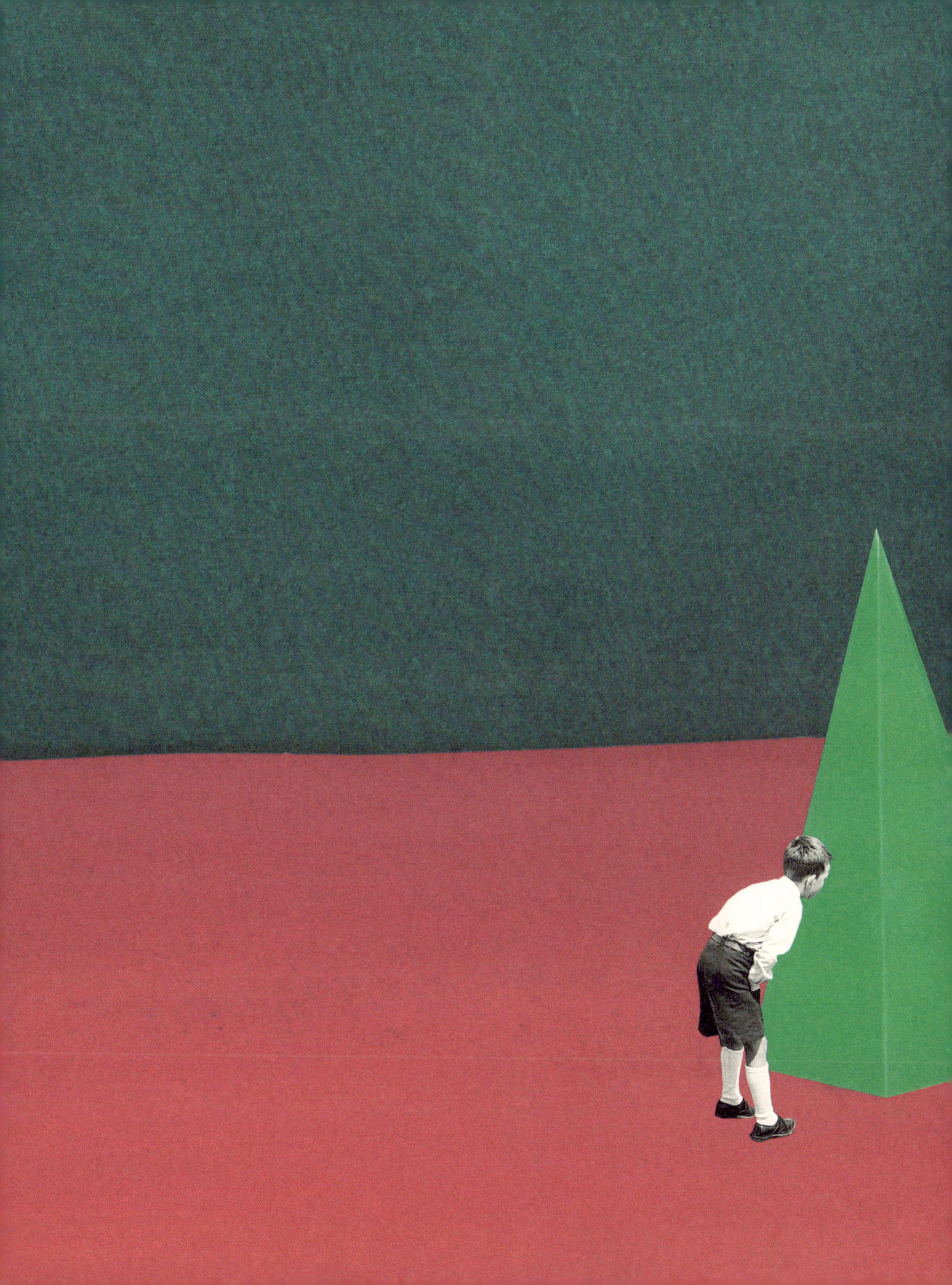

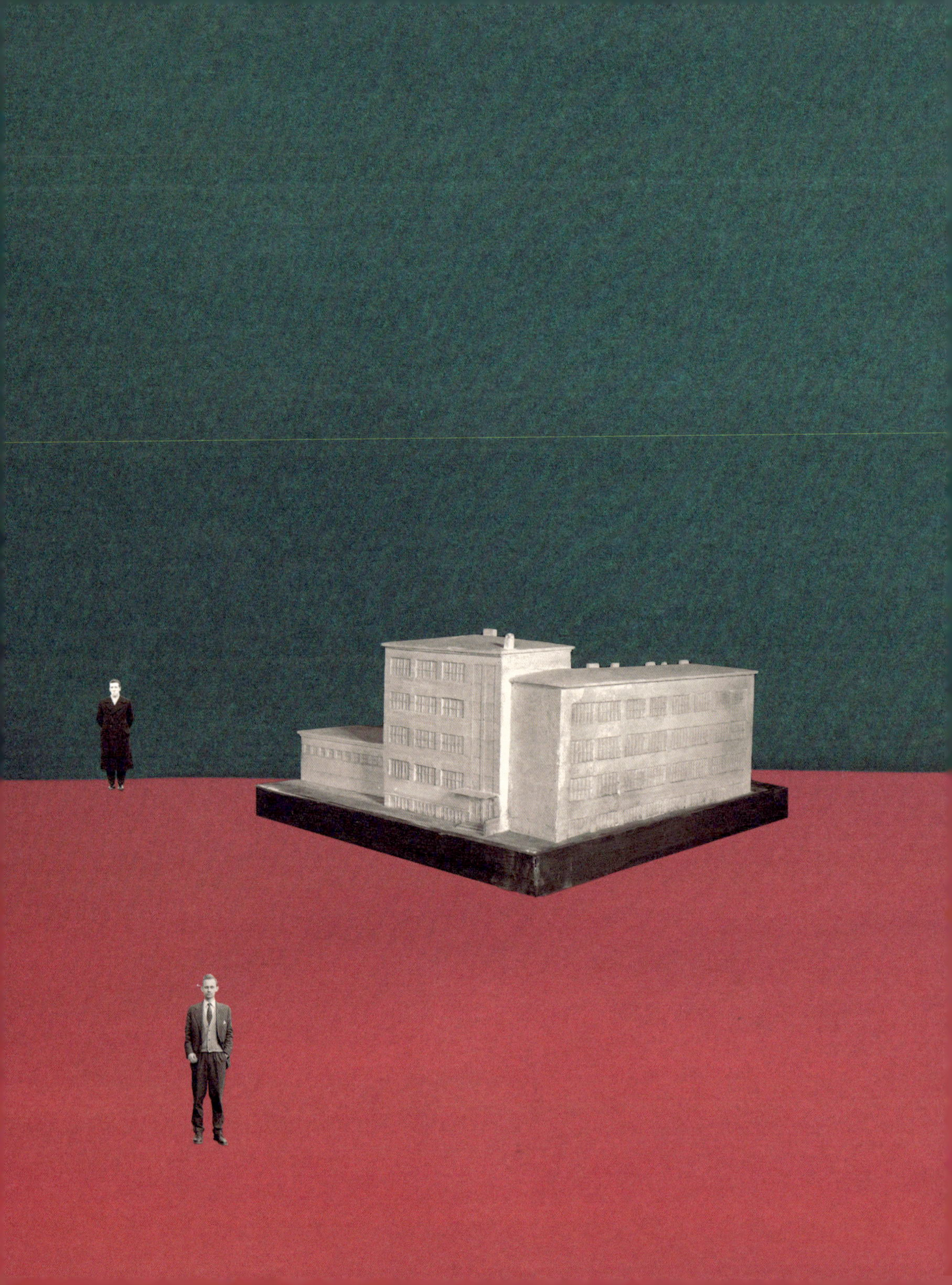

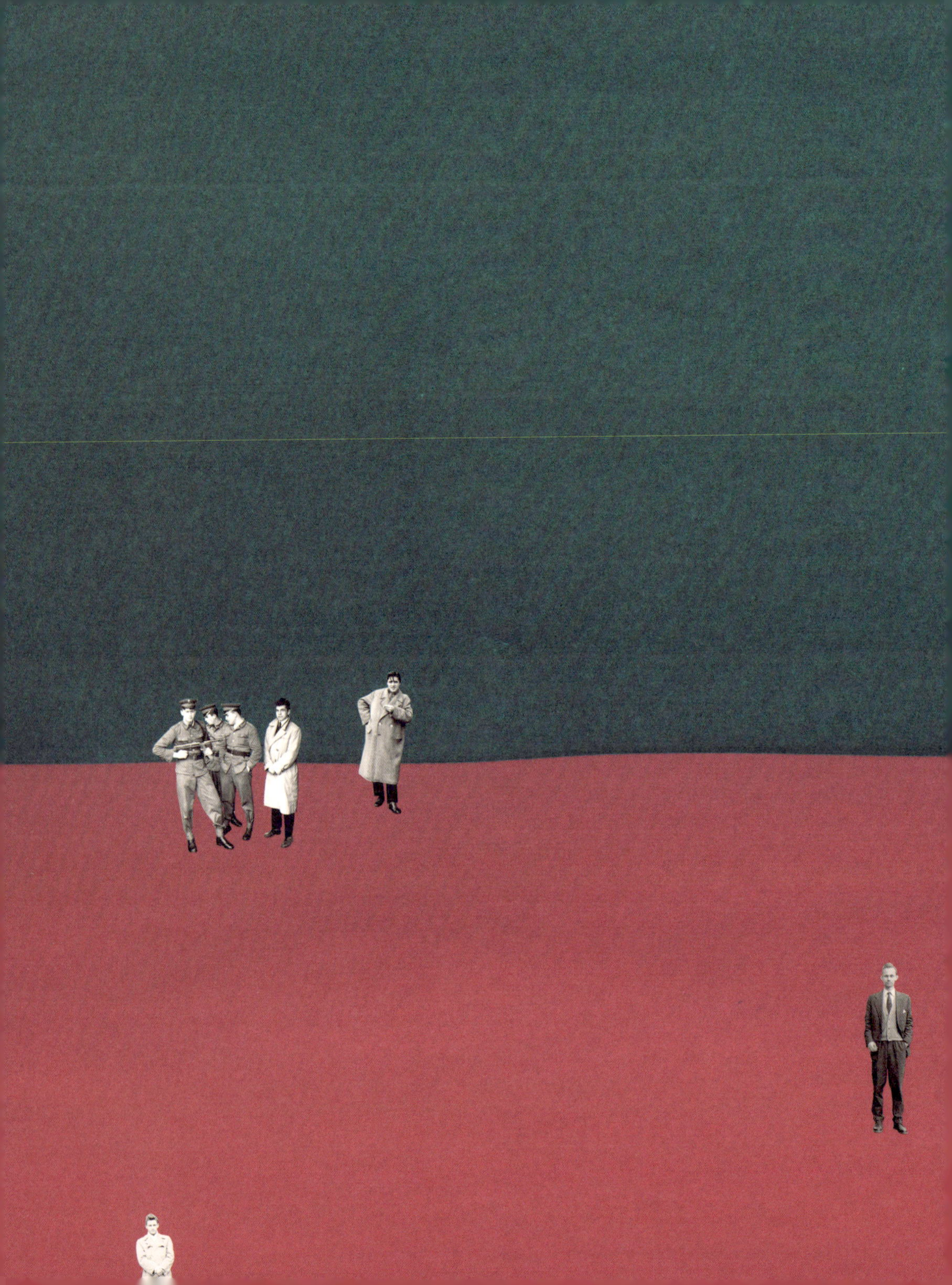

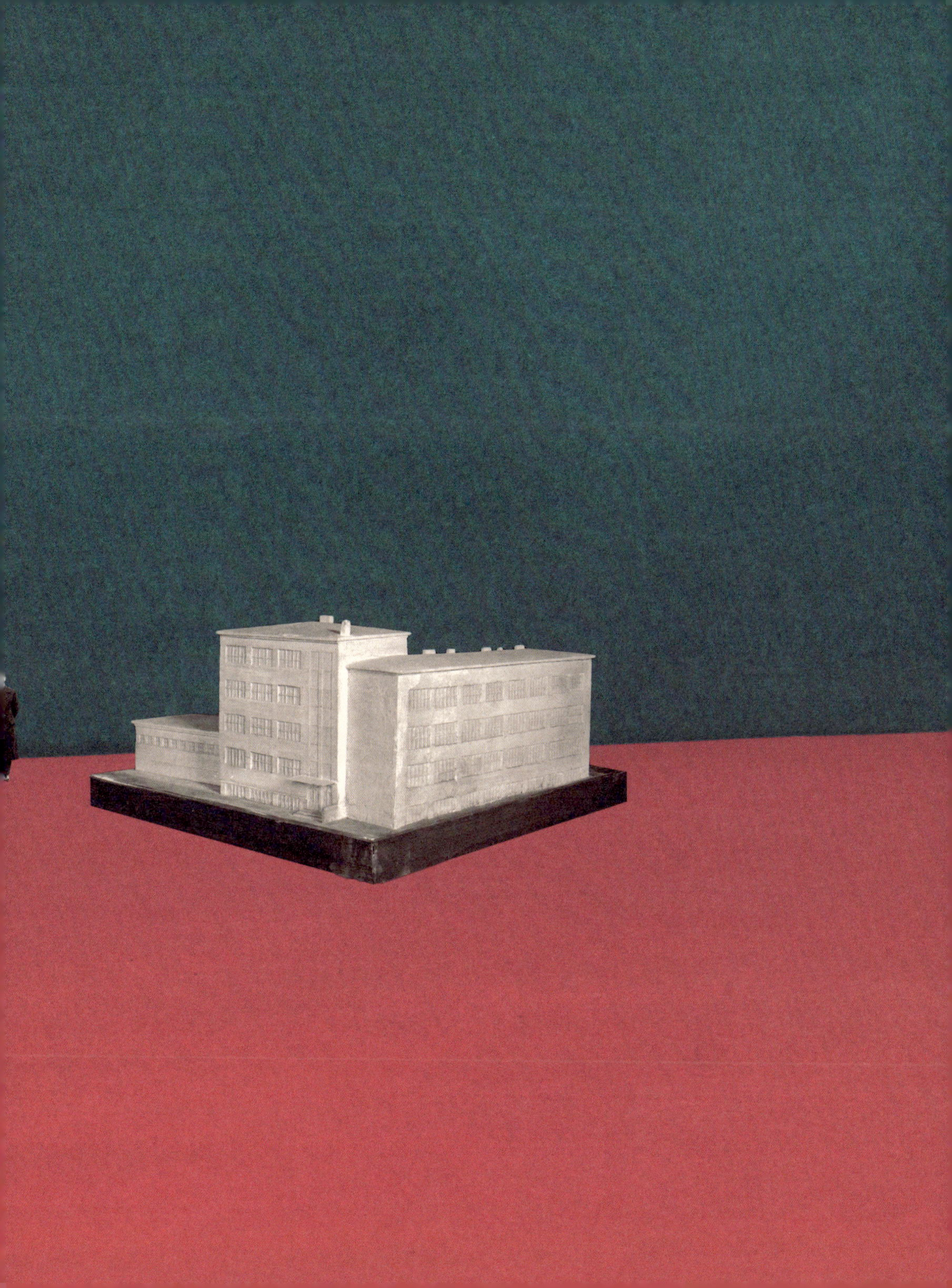

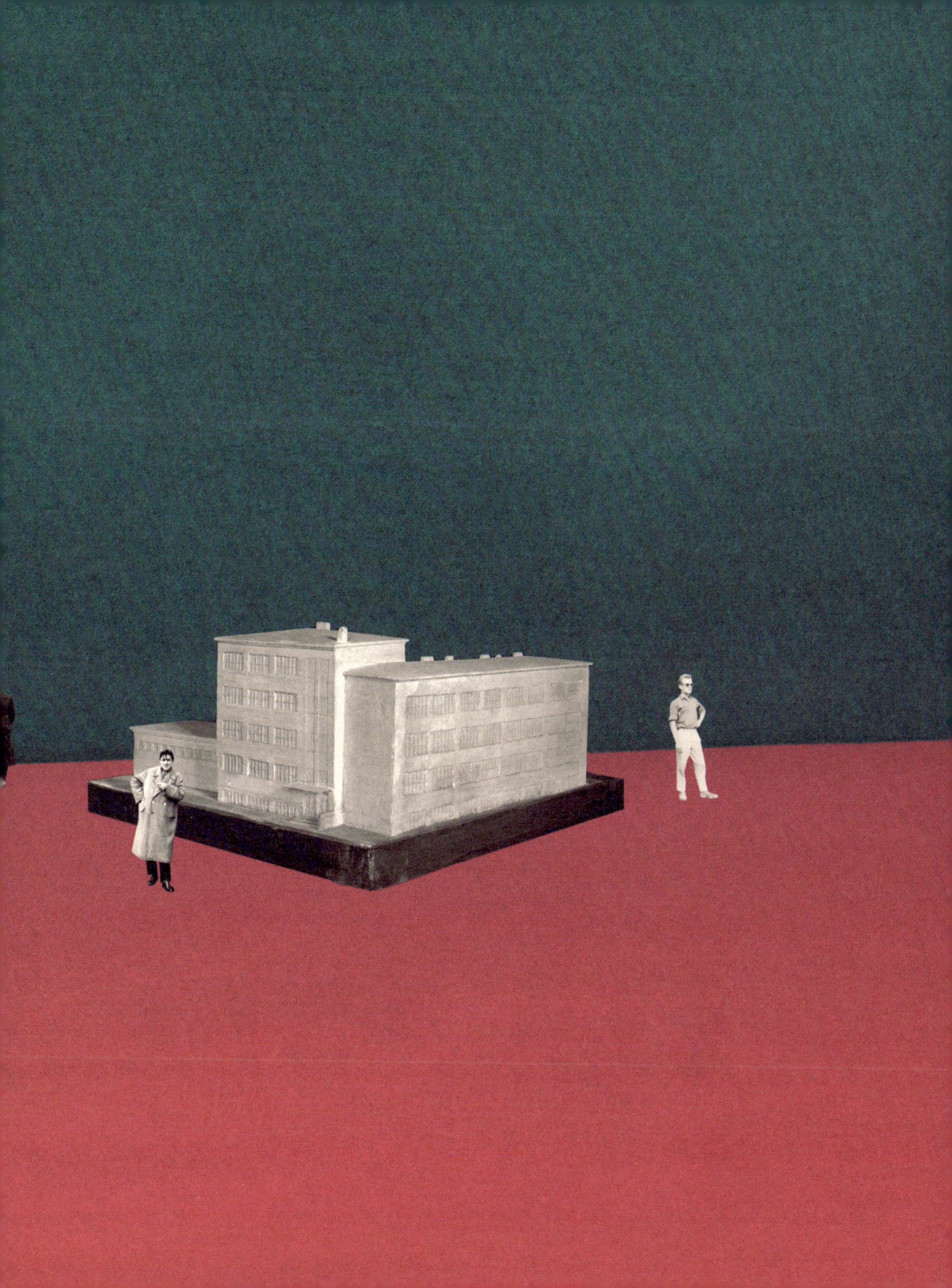

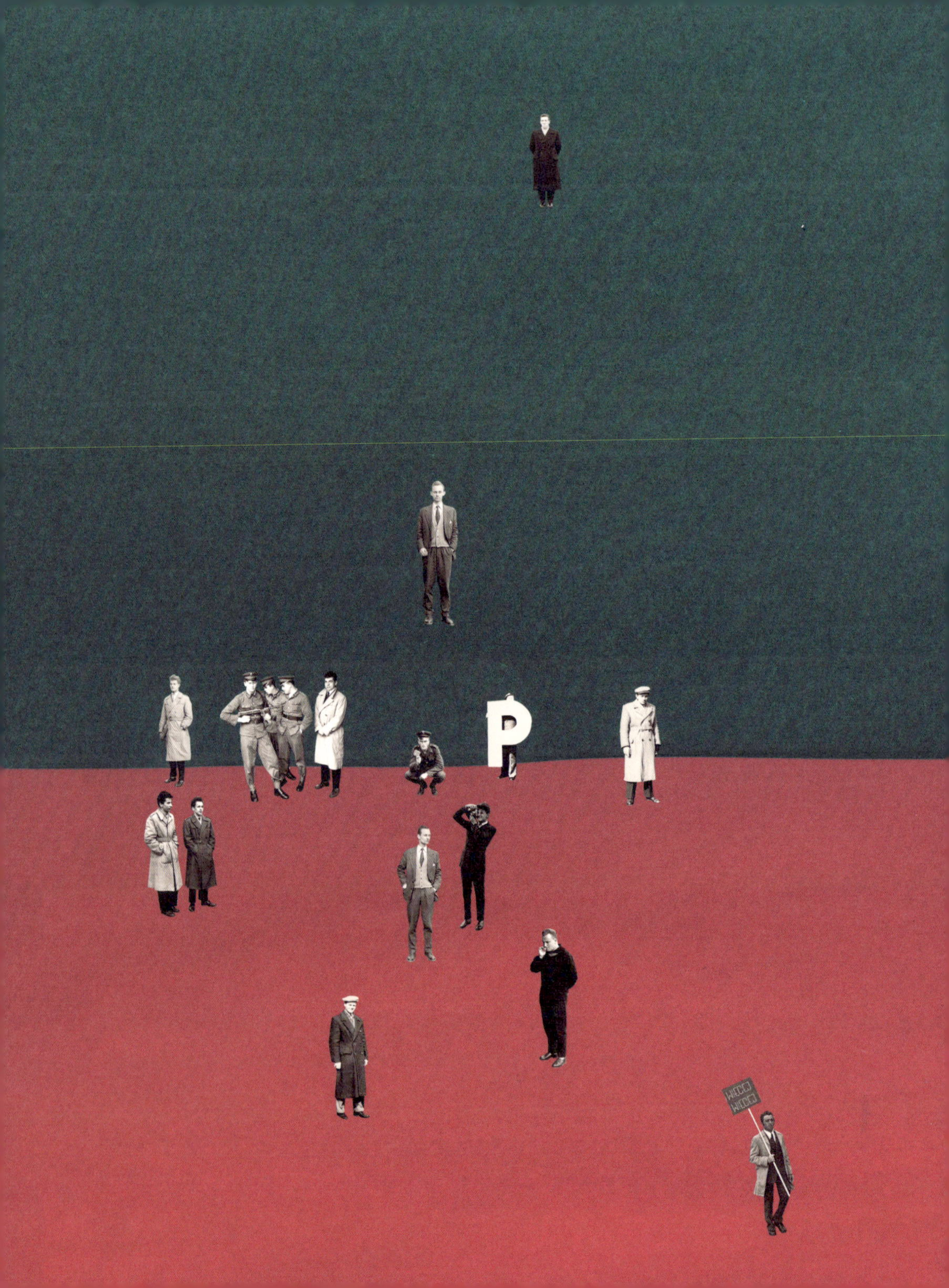

From: **Maciej Pisuk**
To: **Rafal** cc: Rafal
Subject: **letter from Pisuk**
28.01.2017 01:15

One thing that strikes me here is two layers.

The first one is the abstract level of (mathematical and geometrical) ideas, but presented by means of 'infantile' period characters, who are used as teaching aids – they can be treated as elements of the educational system, a system that disciplines and educates citizens. Thus they are symbols of a system in general, one that forces you to accept abstract – though 'scholarly' – ideas. What is important to me is the 'retro' infantility reminiscent of Communist Poland, which is linked to the second level: that of the protagonists in the photographs. They form a distinct group (classmates? friends who met in the army, or rather during compulsory military service – this would be my guess), who keep 'pulling faces,' play the part of respectable citizens (suits and uniforms!). In other words, they parody the social roles assigned to them by the system I refer to above (they are imprisoned in their 'roles'). The collages make good illustrations of Gombrowicz's fiction. In a sense, it is a kind of 'weird comic book' telling a dreamy, oneiric story... I like the time-lapse and the game of tag at the end. The hide-and-seek between people and figures, adulthood and childhood. Here, the children are looking for adults so this can be also seen as a search for childhood... or memories of it.

But interestingly, this anecdotal meaning corresponds in an intriguing way to the purely aesthetic dimension.

That's about it, for now...

From: **Rafal**
To: **Maciej Pisuk**
Subject: **letter from Pisuk**
29.01.2017 13:25

It all happens in Września. At first, I didn't intend to include the 'Września children strike' in the story (a pretty obvious association), but later I started to get used to the idea. The strike materialised in the form of somewhat worn out teaching aids which I photographed in Września's primary and middle schools. When superimposed on each other, the geometrical models formed cages, which are indeed a kind of disciplinary system.

As to the self-satisfied dandies, they come from the archive of the outstanding (in my opinion) photographer Ryszard Szczepaniak. You are right about his relationship with the guys in the photographs: they are friends of his brother and Szczepaniak himself. Szczepaniak created a space for them which removed them from the context. In a sense, he took them out of the system (which, after all, they are part of as regime soldiers and the model elegant citizens you refer to). This could even be taken for an anarchistic gesture.

And what would happen if the happy, well-dressed, and – as I assume – not politically engaged gentlemen were grouped together and activated? Let them stage a demonstration and protest, regardless of the consequences. Let them stop being indifferent.

ACKNOWLEDGMENTS

I would like to thank all the people who shared their private or institutional archives. I wish to extend special thanks to Mr. Ryszard Szczepaniak, whose photographs have been a key source of inspiration in my work. They allowed me to travel back in time to the Września of the 1950s, but more importantly, to meet an outstanding photographer and a wonderful person. I am also grateful to all the collectors, enthusiasts and institutions who gather, save, and archive important documents, notably photographs, illustrating the town's history. These form a lasting visual record of Września, building its identity. When working on the project, I viewed tens of thousands of photographs, which was a true adventure for me. Given the final character of the work, I was not able to include all of them. I would like to thank in particular the following persons for making their archives available: Piotr Lenart, the Grześkowiak Family, Robert Klimczak, Waldemar Śliwczyński and the editors of *Wiadomości Wrzesińskie*, Robert Majewski, Jakub Banaszak and Kornel Tomczak from 'Projekt Września,' Arkadiusz Rychlewski, Władysław Nowicki, The Children of Września Regional Museum, The Fire Service, The Municipal Police, The Commune Office in Września, and The Culture Centre in Września. I would like to thank Primary Schools Nos. 1 and 2, Middle School No. 2, and the Complex of Schools in Otoczna for allowing me to photograph their teaching aids. I thank Kuba Goc for his organisational help. I would like to thank Krzysztof Kowalczyk for his help in my struggle with the text.

I wish to thank my wife Ania, who keeps inspiring me and provides help with each publication I work on. I extend my thanks to Maciej Pisuk for his much appreciated remarks and keeping up the revolutionary spirit. Last but not least, I would like to thank Karol Szymkowiak, the curator of the Września Collection, for inviting me to create Września Collection 2016, and the Town of Września for the exceptional initiative.

ABOUT THE WRZEŚNIA COLLECTION

The Września Collection is a long-term photographic project which works towards creating a photographic archive for the Town and Commune of Września. Every year, Mayor of the Town and Commune of Września Tomasz Kałużny invites one photographer named by the curator to be an artist-in-residence. The task facing the artist is to create a personal set of photographs illustrating the commune and its residents. The photographer is given full artistic freedom, both in choosing the topic, and the method of its presentation. The outcome of his/her work is published in a photobook and exhibited in Września.

Thanks to the Września Collection, the people who live here have the opportunity to look at themselves and the space they live in from the perspective of an artist who is an external observer. The 'external eye' enables them to learn something new about the people, places and phenomena which are so close to them, but often escape their attention in everyday life. The Września Collection is also meant to reach 'outside' – beyond the city where it is created. Thus Września becomes a universal town, with the photographer telling stories that have a much broader context, extending beyond the place where the project is produced, but inherently related to it.

In the future, the collection of photographs will be an invaluable witness of our time. At present, it is meant to discover, provoke reflection, and pose questions. As does *The First March of Gentlemen* by Rafał Milach, whom I invited for the eighth edition of the Września Collection.

Września Collection artists:
Bogdan Konopka (2009), Andrzej Jerzy Lech (2010), Mariusz Forecki (2011), Nicolas Grospierre (2012), Zbigniew Tomaszczuk (2013), Katarzyna Majak (2014), Adam Lach (2015)

Września Collection curators:
Waldemar Śliwczyński (2009–2014), Karol Szymkowiak (since 2015)

Rafał Milach *The First March of Gentlemen*

Collages © Rafał Milach
www.rafalmilach.com
Second edition 2018

Texts © Rafał Milach, Maciej Pisuk, Karol Szymkowiak
Book design © Rafał Milach, Ania Nałęcka-Milach
Translation © Krzysztof Kowalczyk
English version proofreading © Nicholas Hodge
Typeset in Cervo Neue
Printing: Chromapress, Piaseczno
Binding: Poligrafia Bracia Szymańscy, Warszawa
Print run: 650 copies including 50 copies of the special edition
Publisher: © GOST Books

GOST Books
8a West Smithfield
London
EC1A 9JR
info@gostbooks.com
gostbooks.com

British Library cataloguing-in-publication data. A catalogue record of this book is available from the British Library.

ISBN: 978-1-910401-17-0

GOST

The First March of Gentlemen is a result of Września Collection 2016 residency